SELF-CROWNED

JOURNAL

Thank You

2/2/1c

YOUR NEW LIFE STARTS HERE.

by *Derrick Jaxn*

Self-Crowned Journal
ISBN: 978-0-9910336-9-0

selfcrowned.com

WELCOME

You're in the right place. Now, let's do the right thing. Understand that Self-Crowned is not a magic trick. It's a resource and it only works as a complementary piece to your commitment to your self-love. Also understand that each component of this journal is specifically designed to help reinforce the version of yourself that will allow you to live your most fulfilled life regardless of who is in or out of it, what money you do or do not currently have, and regardless of what past experiences convinced you that you would be broken forever.

After completing the Self-Crowned Journal, you will notice yourself holding the keys to your mental and emotional state throughout the day in moments you formerly would have turned over to whoever it was you last loved that decided to pop back up on your mind. You'll notice the frustrations that used to consume you simply don't anymore, and the people who used to drain you won't feel comfortable remaining in your presence while those looking to pour into you will be drawn to you and want to stick around long-term. This is the proven power of the exercises within these pages, but they only work if you truly commit to them.

It's time to turn your mindset around, rediscover your happiness, and attract every blessing that already has your name on it. Let's do it, together.

INSTRUCTIONS

 **Every day, you're going to start your morning by writing out an affirmation** for what it is you deserve or identify within yourself as already having as an intrinsic quality. One example may be, "I am beautiful, and it's obvious to everyone who deserves to see it." Another example would be, "I'm capable of accomplishing every goal that's been placed upon my heart."

 **From that affirmation, follow through the rest of the page as outlined, without skipping a single portion.** The meditation is most effective when your phone notifications are turned off or completely out of reach, and there's soft music to help create a peaceful atmosphere around you. The intent is to completely immerse yourself in the visualization of the materialization of the goals you wrote down as well as your affirmation being put on full display. Allow yourself to feel the joy and gratitude of seeing those things come full circle, and even the reaction by those who will see them, too. If you've never meditated before, this may be uncomfortable at first, but the rewards are tremendous!

 **Entries don't have to be elaborate or perfect,** but you must absolutely mean them as this will become a regular reference for the future, and possibly years to come.

 **After completing each week of entries, you'll then complete your weekly score card.** Take the time out for yourself, no matter how busy your life is, to dedicate yourself to this as well as the rest of the journal. This is a life-changing process from the inside out, and you deserve the space to dedicate yourself to it.

Without further ado, let's get started!

TODAY'S AFFIRMATION:

The power of my future is greater than the pain of my past.

THREE THINGS YOU ARE GRATEFUL FOR AND WHY:

Health - Being sick is miserable & scary
Freedom - I'm allowed to live life on my terms
Parents - A lot of people don't have theirs

ONE GOAL YOU'D LIKE TO ACCOMPLISH TODAY (EMOTIONAL OR MENTAL STATE):

Today. I will not allow anyone to make me defensive. no matter how wrong they are.

Spend 15-20 minutes in meditation on the things you just wrote. _Initial here when you're done._ _PJ_

Spend at least 30 minutes consuming positive media (inspirational podcasts, books, videos, etc.). _Initial here when you're done._ _PJ_

♛ NIGHTLY SELF-CARE INVESTMENT

Describe an instance where someone or something attempted to take control of your energy and you did _not_ allow it. etc.).
Initial here when you're done. _PJ_

ONE THING YOU'RE PROUD OF YOURSELF FOR DOING TODAY IS:

Ended or avoided every conversation that led me to feeling defensive

NOTE: Shut down all social media, TVs, and Netflix at least two hours before bed. Your mind being able to slow down before you go to sleep is critical to its ability to effectively recharge and handle the tasks of the next day.

WEEKLY SCORE CARD

WROTE DOWN AFFIRMATION

Yes : 7 /7 = _100%_

| MON | TUES | WED | THURS | FRI | SAT | SUN |

WROTE DOWN GOALS

Yes : 7 /7 = _100%_

| MON | TUES | WED | THURS | FRI | SAT | SUN |

MEDITATED FOR FULL 15-20 MINUTES

Yes : 7 /7 = _100%_

| MON | TUES | WED | THURS | FRI | SAT | SUN |

CONSUMED POSITIVE MEDIA
FOR FULL 30+ MINUTES

Yes : 7 /7 = _100%_

| MON | TUES | WED | THURS | FRI | SAT | SUN |

COMPLETED NIGHTLY SELF-CARE

Yes : 7 /7 = _100%_

| MON | TUES | WED | THURS | FRI | SAT | SUN |

THURSDAY

I am realigned with my soul
and compassionate towards myself
+ others

WEEK 1

MONDAY

→ SKIP TO
FRI →

TODAY'S AFFIRMATION:

I am realigned with my soul
and compassionate towards myself
& others

THREE THINGS YOU ARE GRATEFUL FOR AND WHY:

Healthy food + safe, warm home; it's a gift
My health; It's the biggest gift
and not granted.
All the great opportunities - I'm on the
right path

**ONE GOAL YOU'D LIKE TO ACCOMPLISH TODAY
(EMOTIONAL OR MENTAL STATE):**

Stay compassionate and loving
towards self

Spend 15-20 minutes in meditation on the things you just wrote.
Initial here when you're done. MH

Spend at least 30 minutes consuming positive media (inspirational podcasts,
books, videos, etc.). *Initial here when you're done.* MH

♛ NIGHTLY SELF-CARE INVESTMENT

Describe an instance where someone or something attempted to take control
of your energy and you did *not* allow it. etc.).
Initial here when you're done. MH

ONE THING YOU'RE PROUD OF YOURSELF FOR DOING TODAY IS:

I stayed centered + finished every-
thing

NOTE: Shut down all social media, TVs, and Netflix at least two hours before bed.
Your mind being able to slow down before you go to sleep is critical to its ability to
effectively recharge and handle the tasks of the next day.

TODAY'S AFFIRMATION:

_____

_____

THREE THINGS YOU ARE GRATEFUL FOR AND WHY:

_____

_____

_____

ONE GOAL YOU'D LIKE TO ACCOMPLISH TODAY
(EMOTIONAL OR MENTAL STATE):

_____

_____

Spend 15-20 minutes in meditation on the things you just wrote.
Initial here when you're done. _____

Spend at least 30 minutes consuming positive media (inspirational podcasts,
books, videos, etc.). *Initial here when you're done.* _____

NIGHTLY SELF-CARE INVESTMENT

Describe an instance where someone or something attempted to take control
of your energy and you did *not* allow it. etc.).
Initial here when you're done. _____

ONE THING YOU'RE PROUD OF YOURSELF FOR DOING TODAY IS:

_____

NOTE: Shut down all social media, TVs, and Netflix at least two hours before bed.
Your mind being able to slow down before you go to sleep is critical to its ability to
effectively recharge and handle the tasks of the next day.

WEDNESDAY

TODAY'S AFFIRMATION:

_____

_____

THREE THINGS YOU ARE GRATEFUL FOR AND WHY:

_____

_____

_____

ONE GOAL YOU'D LIKE TO ACCOMPLISH TODAY
(EMOTIONAL OR MENTAL STATE):

_____

_____

Spend 15-20 minutes in meditation on the things you just wrote.
Initial here when you're done. _____

Spend at least 30 minutes consuming positive media (inspirational podcasts,
books, videos, etc.). _Initial here when you're done._ _____

NIGHTLY SELF-CARE INVESTMENT

Describe an instance where someone or something attempted to take control
of your energy and you did **not** allow it. etc.).
Initial here when you're done. _____

ONE THING YOU'RE PROUD OF YOURSELF FOR DOING TODAY IS:

_____

NOTE: Shut down all social media, TVs, and Netflix at least two hours before bed.
Your mind being able to slow down before you go to sleep is critical to its ability to
effectively recharge and handle the tasks of the next day.

TODAY'S AFFIRMATION:

_____

_____

THREE THINGS YOU ARE GRATEFUL FOR AND WHY:

_____

_____

_____

ONE GOAL YOU'D LIKE TO ACCOMPLISH TODAY
(EMOTIONAL OR MENTAL STATE):

_____

_____

Spend 15-20 minutes in meditation on the things you just wrote.
Initial here when you're done. _____

Spend at least 30 minutes consuming positive media (inspirational podcasts, books, videos, etc.). *Initial here when you're done.* _____

NIGHTLY SELF-CARE INVESTMENT

Describe an instance where someone or something attempted to take control of your energy and you did *not* allow it. etc.).
Initial here when you're done. _____

ONE THING YOU'RE PROUD OF YOURSELF FOR DOING TODAY IS:

_____

NOTE: Shut down all social media, TVs, and Netflix at least two hours before bed. Your mind being able to slow down before you go to sleep is critical to its ability to effectively recharge and handle the tasks of the next day.

FRIDAY

TODAY'S AFFIRMATION:

Love and compassion
is in me and out

THREE THINGS YOU ARE GRATEFUL FOR AND WHY:

ONE GOAL YOU'D LIKE TO ACCOMPLISH TODAY
(EMOTIONAL OR MENTAL STATE):

I kept the loving
compassion on ♡

Spend 15-20 minutes in meditation on the things you just wrote.
Initial here when you're done. _____

Spend at least 30 minutes consuming positive media (inspirational podcasts,
books, videos, etc.). _Initial here when you're done._ _____

NIGHTLY SELF-CARE INVESTMENT

Describe an instance where someone or something attempted to take control
of your energy and you did **_not_** allow it. etc.).
Initial here when you're done. _____

ONE THING YOU'RE PROUD OF YOURSELF FOR DOING TODAY IS:

I stayed with the feeling

NOTE: Shut down all social media, TVs, and Netflix at least two hours before bed.
Your mind being able to slow down before you go to sleep is critical to its ability to
effectively recharge and handle the tasks of the next day.

TODAY'S AFFIRMATION:

I am beautiful, glowing in & out, & it's visible

THREE THINGS YOU ARE GRATEFUL FOR AND WHY:

_____

_____

_____

ONE GOAL YOU'D LIKE TO ACCOMPLISH TODAY
(EMOTIONAL OR MENTAL STATE):

_____

_____

Spend 15-20 minutes in meditation on the things you just wrote.
Initial here when you're done. _____

Spend at least 30 minutes consuming positive media (inspirational podcasts,
books, videos, etc.). *Initial here when you're done* _____

NIGHTLY SELF-CARE INVESTMENT

Describe an instance where someone or something attempted to take control
of your energy and you did *not* allow it. etc.).
Initial here when you're done _____

ONE THING YOU'RE PROUD OF YOURSELF FOR DOING TODAY IS:

I felt peaceful + stayed in kindness

NOTE: Shut down all social media, TVs, and Netflix at least two hours before bed.
Your mind being able to slow down before you go to sleep is critical to its ability to
effectively recharge and handle the tasks of the next day.

SUNDAY

TODAY'S AFFIRMATION:

_____

_____

THREE THINGS YOU ARE GRATEFUL FOR AND WHY:

_____

_____

_____

ONE GOAL YOU'D LIKE TO ACCOMPLISH TODAY
(EMOTIONAL OR MENTAL STATE):

_____

_____

Spend 15-20 minutes in meditation on the things you just wrote.
Initial here when you're done. _____

Spend at least 30 minutes consuming positive media (inspirational podcasts,
books, videos, etc.). _Initial here when you're done._ _____

NIGHTLY SELF-CARE INVESTMENT

Describe an instance where someone or something attempted to take control
of your energy and you did **not** allow it. etc.).
Initial here when you're done. _____

ONE THING YOU'RE PROUD OF YOURSELF FOR DOING TODAY IS:

_____

NOTE: Shut down all social media, TVs, and Netflix at least two hours before bed.
Your mind being able to slow down before you go to sleep is critical to its ability to
effectively recharge and handle the tasks of the next day.

WEEKLY SCORE CARD

WROTE DOWN AFFIRMATION

_____: ____/7 =

MON   TUES   WED   THURS   FRI   SAT   SUN

WROTE DOWN GOALS

_____: ____/7 =

MON   TUES   WED   THURS   FRI   SAT   SUN

MEDITATED FOR FULL 15-20 MINUTES

_____: ____/7 =

MON   TUES   WED   THURS   FRI   SAT   SUN

CONSUMED POSITIVE MEDIA FOR FULL 30+ MINUTES

_____: ____/7 =

MON   TUES   WED   THURS   FRI   SAT   SUN

COMPLETED NIGHTLY SELF-CARE

_____: ____/7 =

MON   TUES   WED   THURS   FRI   SAT   SUN

WEEKLY SCORE CARD

WHAT HELPED YOU ACHIEVE 100% ON ALL SELF-LOVE INVESTMENTS, AND IF YOU DIDN'T, WHAT DO YOU BELIEVE HINDERED YOU?

I kept track of my thoughts, I was focused

WHAT WILL YOU DO TO ACHIEVE 100% NEXT WEEK?

I will keep on doing what I did, with love ♡

MAJOR TAKEAWAY FROM THIS PAST WEEK THAT YOU'VE LEARNED ABOUT YOURSELF OR LIFE IN GENERAL?

Kindness always pays off

ONE THING THAT HELPS YOU FEEL YOUR ABSOLUTE BEST THIS PAST WEEK:

Compassion

ONE THING THAT MADE YOU FEEL NOT SO GREAT THIS PAST WEEK:

Foggy brain + tiredness

NAME A WAY YOU WILL CONQUER THAT THING THAT PREVENTED YOU FROM FEELING YOUR BEST.

Rest

WEEK 2

MONDAY

TODAY'S AFFIRMATION:

_____

_____

THREE THINGS YOU ARE GRATEFUL FOR AND WHY:

_____

_____

_____

ONE GOAL YOU'D LIKE TO ACCOMPLISH TODAY
(EMOTIONAL OR MENTAL STATE):

_____

_____

Spend 15-20 minutes in meditation on the things you just wrote.
Initial here when you're done. _____

Spend at least 30 minutes consuming positive media (inspirational podcasts,
books, videos, etc.). _Initial here when you're done._ _____

NIGHTLY SELF-CARE INVESTMENT

Describe an instance where someone or something attempted to take control
of your energy and you did **not** allow it. etc.).
Initial here when you're done. _____

ONE THING YOU'RE PROUD OF YOURSELF FOR DOING TODAY IS:

_____

NOTE: Shut down all social media, TVs, and Netflix at least two hours before bed.
Your mind being able to slow down before you go to sleep is critical to its ability to
effectively recharge and handle the tasks of the next day.

TODAY'S AFFIRMATION:

_____

_____

THREE THINGS YOU ARE GRATEFUL FOR AND WHY:

_____

_____

_____

ONE GOAL YOU'D LIKE TO ACCOMPLISH TODAY
(EMOTIONAL OR MENTAL STATE):

_____

_____

Spend 15-20 minutes in meditation on the things you just wrote.
Initial here when you're done. _____

Spend at least 30 minutes consuming positive media (inspirational podcasts,
books, videos, etc.). *Initial here when you're done.* _____

NIGHTLY SELF-CARE INVESTMENT

Describe an instance where someone or something attempted to take control
of your energy and you did *not* allow it. etc.).
Initial here when you're done. _____

ONE THING YOU'RE PROUD OF YOURSELF FOR DOING TODAY IS:

_____

NOTE: Shut down all social media, TVs, and Netflix at least two hours before bed.
Your mind being able to slow down before you go to sleep is critical to its ability to
effectively recharge and handle the tasks of the next day.

WEDNESDAY

TODAY'S AFFIRMATION:

_____

_____

THREE THINGS YOU ARE GRATEFUL FOR AND WHY:

_____

_____

_____

ONE GOAL YOU'D LIKE TO ACCOMPLISH TODAY
(EMOTIONAL OR MENTAL STATE):

_____

_____

Spend 15-20 minutes in meditation on the things you just wrote.
Initial here when you're done. _____

Spend at least 30 minutes consuming positive media (inspirational podcasts,
books, videos, etc.). *Initial here when you're done.* _____

NIGHTLY SELF-CARE INVESTMENT

Describe an instance where someone or something attempted to take control
of your energy and you did *not* allow it. etc.).
Initial here when you're done. _____

ONE THING YOU'RE PROUD OF YOURSELF FOR DOING TODAY IS:

_____

NOTE: Shut down all social media, TVs, and Netflix at least two hours before bed.
Your mind being able to slow down before you go to sleep is critical to its ability to
effectively recharge and handle the tasks of the next day.

TODAY'S AFFIRMATION:

_____

_____

THREE THINGS YOU ARE GRATEFUL FOR AND WHY:

_____

_____

_____

ONE GOAL YOU'D LIKE TO ACCOMPLISH TODAY
(EMOTIONAL OR MENTAL STATE):

_____

_____

Spend 15-20 minutes in meditation on the things you just wrote.
Initial here when you're done. _____

Spend at least 30 minutes consuming positive media (inspirational podcasts, books, videos, etc.). *Initial here when you're done.* _____

NIGHTLY SELF-CARE INVESTMENT

Describe an instance where someone or something attempted to take control of your energy and you did *not* allow it. etc.).
Initial here when you're done. _____

ONE THING YOU'RE PROUD OF YOURSELF FOR DOING TODAY IS:

_____

NOTE: Shut down all social media, TVs, and Netflix at least two hours before bed. Your mind being able to slow down before you go to sleep is critical to its ability to effectively recharge and handle the tasks of the next day.

FRIDAY

TODAY'S AFFIRMATION:

_____

_____

THREE THINGS YOU ARE GRATEFUL FOR AND WHY:

_____

_____

_____

ONE GOAL YOU'D LIKE TO ACCOMPLISH TODAY
(EMOTIONAL OR MENTAL STATE):

_____

_____

Spend 15-20 minutes in meditation on the things you just wrote.
Initial here when you're done. _____

Spend at least 30 minutes consuming positive media (inspirational podcasts,
books, videos, etc.). _Initial here when you're done._ _____

NIGHTLY SELF-CARE INVESTMENT

Describe an instance where someone or something attempted to take control
of your energy and you did **_not_** allow it. etc.).
Initial here when you're done. _____

ONE THING YOU'RE PROUD OF YOURSELF FOR DOING TODAY IS:

_____

NOTE: Shut down all social media, TVs, and Netflix at least two hours before bed.
Your mind being able to slow down before you go to sleep is critical to its ability to
effectively recharge and handle the tasks of the next day.

SATURDAY

TODAY'S AFFIRMATION:

_____

_____

THREE THINGS YOU ARE GRATEFUL FOR AND WHY:

_____

_____

_____

ONE GOAL YOU'D LIKE TO ACCOMPLISH TODAY
(EMOTIONAL OR MENTAL STATE):

_____

_____

Spend 15-20 minutes in meditation on the things you just wrote.
Initial here when you're done. _____

Spend at least 30 minutes consuming positive media (inspirational podcasts,
books, videos, etc.). *Initial here when you're done.* _____

👑 NIGHTLY SELF-CARE INVESTMENT

Describe an instance where someone or something attempted to take control
of your energy and you did *not* allow it. etc.).
Initial here when you're done. _____

ONE THING YOU'RE PROUD OF YOURSELF FOR DOING TODAY IS:

_____

NOTE: Shut down all social media, TVs, and Netflix at least two hours before bed.
Your mind being able to slow down before you go to sleep is critical to its ability to
effectively recharge and handle the tasks of the next day.

SUNDAY

TODAY'S AFFIRMATION:

_____

_____

THREE THINGS YOU ARE GRATEFUL FOR AND WHY:

_____

_____

_____

ONE GOAL YOU'D LIKE TO ACCOMPLISH TODAY
(EMOTIONAL OR MENTAL STATE):

_____

_____

Spend 15-20 minutes in meditation on the things you just wrote.
Initial here when you're done. _____

Spend at least 30 minutes consuming positive media (inspirational podcasts,
books, videos, etc.). _Initial here when you're done._ _____

NIGHTLY SELF-CARE INVESTMENT

Describe an instance where someone or something attempted to take control
of your energy and you did **not** allow it. etc.).
Initial here when you're done. _____

ONE THING YOU'RE PROUD OF YOURSELF FOR DOING TODAY IS:

_____

NOTE: Shut down all social media, TVs, and Netflix at least two hours before bed.
Your mind being able to slow down before you go to sleep is critical to its ability to
effectively recharge and handle the tasks of the next day.

WEEKLY SCORE CARD

WROTE DOWN AFFIRMATION

_____: ____/7 =

MON TUES WED THURS FRI SAT SUN

WROTE DOWN GOALS

_____: ____/7 =

MON TUES WED THURS FRI SAT SUN

MEDITATED FOR FULL 15-20 MINUTES

_____: ____/7 =

MON TUES WED THURS FRI SAT SUN

CONSUMED POSITIVE MEDIA FOR FULL 30+ MINUTES

_____: ____/7 =

MON TUES WED THURS FRI SAT SUN

COMPLETED NIGHTLY SELF-CARE

_____: ____/7 =

MON TUES WED THURS FRI SAT SUN

WEEKLY SCORE CARD

WHAT HELPED YOU ACHIEVE 100% ON ALL SELF-LOVE INVESTMENTS, AND IF YOU DIDN'T, WHAT DO YOU BELIEVE HINDERED YOU?

_____

_____

WHAT WILL YOU DO TO ACHIEVE 100% NEXT WEEK?

_____

_____

MAJOR TAKEAWAY FROM THIS PAST WEEK THAT YOU'VE LEARNED ABOUT YOURSELF OR LIFE IN GENERAL?

_____

_____

ONE THING THAT HELPS YOU FEEL YOUR ABSOLUTE BEST THIS PAST WEEK:

_____

_____

ONE THING THAT MADE YOU FEEL NOT SO GREAT THIS PAST WEEK:

_____

_____

NAME A WAY YOU WILL CONQUER THAT THING THAT PREVENTED YOU FROM FEELING YOUR BEST.

_____

_____

WEEK 3

MONDAY

TODAY'S AFFIRMATION:

_____

_____

THREE THINGS YOU ARE GRATEFUL FOR AND WHY:

_____

_____

_____

ONE GOAL YOU'D LIKE TO ACCOMPLISH TODAY
(EMOTIONAL OR MENTAL STATE):

_____

_____

Spend 15-20 minutes in meditation on the things you just wrote.
Initial here when you're done. _____

Spend at least 30 minutes consuming positive media (inspirational podcasts,
books, videos, etc.). *Initial here when you're done.* _____

👑 NIGHTLY SELF-CARE INVESTMENT

Describe an instance where someone or something attempted to take control
of your energy and you did **not** allow it. etc.).
Initial here when you're done. _____

ONE THING YOU'RE PROUD OF YOURSELF FOR DOING TODAY IS:

_____

NOTE: Shut down all social media, TVs, and Netflix at least two hours before bed.
Your mind being able to slow down before you go to sleep is critical to its ability to
effectively recharge and handle the tasks of the next day.

TUESDAY

TODAY'S AFFIRMATION:

_____

_____

THREE THINGS YOU ARE GRATEFUL FOR AND WHY:

_____

_____

_____

ONE GOAL YOU'D LIKE TO ACCOMPLISH TODAY
(EMOTIONAL OR MENTAL STATE):

_____

_____

Spend 15-20 minutes in meditation on the things you just wrote.
Initial here when you're done. _____

Spend at least 30 minutes consuming positive media (inspirational podcasts,
books, videos, etc.). *Initial here when you're done.* _____

NIGHTLY SELF-CARE INVESTMENT

Describe an instance where someone or something attempted to take control
of your energy and you did **not** allow it. etc.).
Initial here when you're done. _____

ONE THING YOU'RE PROUD OF YOURSELF FOR DOING TODAY IS:

_____

NOTE: Shut down all social media, TVs, and Netflix at least two hours before bed.
Your mind being able to slow down before you go to sleep is critical to its ability to
effectively recharge and handle the tasks of the next day.

WEDNESDAY

TODAY'S AFFIRMATION:

_____

_____

THREE THINGS YOU ARE GRATEFUL FOR AND WHY:

_____

_____

_____

ONE GOAL YOU'D LIKE TO ACCOMPLISH TODAY
(EMOTIONAL OR MENTAL STATE):

_____

_____

Spend 15-20 minutes in meditation on the things you just wrote.
Initial here when you're done. _____

Spend at least 30 minutes consuming positive media (inspirational podcasts,
books, videos, etc.). _Initial here when you're done._ _____

NIGHTLY SELF-CARE INVESTMENT

Describe an instance where someone or something attempted to take control
of your energy and you did **not** allow it. etc.).
Initial here when you're done. _____

ONE THING YOU'RE PROUD OF YOURSELF FOR DOING TODAY IS:

_____

NOTE: Shut down all social media, TVs, and Netflix at least two hours before bed.
Your mind being able to slow down before you go to sleep is critical to its ability to
effectively recharge and handle the tasks of the next day.

THURSDAY

TODAY'S AFFIRMATION:

_____

_____

THREE THINGS YOU ARE GRATEFUL FOR AND WHY:

_____

_____

_____

ONE GOAL YOU'D LIKE TO ACCOMPLISH TODAY
(EMOTIONAL OR MENTAL STATE):

_____

_____

Spend 15-20 minutes in meditation on the things you just wrote.
Initial here when you're done. _____

Spend at least 30 minutes consuming positive media (inspirational podcasts,
books, videos, etc.). _Initial here when you're done._ _____

NIGHTLY SELF-CARE INVESTMENT

Describe an instance where someone or something attempted to take control
of your energy and you did **not** allow it. etc.).
Initial here when you're done. _____

ONE THING YOU'RE PROUD OF YOURSELF FOR DOING TODAY IS:

_____

NOTE: Shut down all social media, TVs, and Netflix at least two hours before bed.
Your mind being able to slow down before you go to sleep is critical to its ability to
effectively recharge and handle the tasks of the next day.

FRIDAY

TODAY'S AFFIRMATION:

_____

_____

THREE THINGS YOU ARE GRATEFUL FOR AND WHY:

_____

_____

_____

ONE GOAL YOU'D LIKE TO ACCOMPLISH TODAY
(EMOTIONAL OR MENTAL STATE):

_____

_____

Spend 15-20 minutes in meditation on the things you just wrote.
Initial here when you're done. _____

Spend at least 30 minutes consuming positive media (inspirational podcasts,
books, videos, etc.). *Initial here when you're done.* _____

NIGHTLY SELF-CARE INVESTMENT

Describe an instance where someone or something attempted to take control
of your energy and you did *not* allow it. etc.).
Initial here when you're done. _____

ONE THING YOU'RE PROUD OF YOURSELF FOR DOING TODAY IS:

_____

NOTE: Shut down all social media, TVs, and Netflix at least two hours before bed.
Your mind being able to slow down before you go to sleep is critical to its ability to
effectively recharge and handle the tasks of the next day.

TODAY'S AFFIRMATION:

_____

_____

THREE THINGS YOU ARE GRATEFUL FOR AND WHY:

_____

_____

_____

ONE GOAL YOU'D LIKE TO ACCOMPLISH TODAY
(EMOTIONAL OR MENTAL STATE):

_____

_____

Spend 15-20 minutes in meditation on the things you just wrote.
Initial here when you're done. _____

Spend at least 30 minutes consuming positive media (inspirational podcasts,
books, videos, etc.). *Initial here when you're done.* _____

NIGHTLY SELF-CARE INVESTMENT

Describe an instance where someone or something attempted to take control
of your energy and you did ***not*** allow it. etc.).
Initial here when you're done. _____

ONE THING YOU'RE PROUD OF YOURSELF FOR DOING TODAY IS:

_____

NOTE: Shut down all social media, TVs, and Netflix at least two hours before bed.
Your mind being able to slow down before you go to sleep is critical to its ability to
effectively recharge and handle the tasks of the next day.

SUNDAY

TODAY'S AFFIRMATION:

_____

_____

THREE THINGS YOU ARE GRATEFUL FOR AND WHY:

_____

_____

_____

ONE GOAL YOU'D LIKE TO ACCOMPLISH TODAY
(EMOTIONAL OR MENTAL STATE):

_____

_____

Spend 15-20 minutes in meditation on the things you just wrote.
Initial here when you're done. _____

Spend at least 30 minutes consuming positive media (inspirational podcasts,
books, videos, etc.). _Initial here when you're done._ _____

NIGHTLY SELF-CARE INVESTMENT

Describe an instance where someone or something attempted to take control
of your energy and you did **not** allow it. etc.).
Initial here when you're done. _____

ONE THING YOU'RE PROUD OF YOURSELF FOR DOING TODAY IS:

_____

NOTE: Shut down all social media, TVs, and Netflix at least two hours before bed.
Your mind being able to slow down before you go to sleep is critical to its ability to
effectively recharge and handle the tasks of the next day.

WEEKLY SCORE CARD

WROTE DOWN AFFIRMATION

_____: ____/7 =

MON   TUES   WED   THURS   FRI   SAT   SUN

WROTE DOWN GOALS

_____: ____/7 =

MON   TUES   WED   THURS   FRI   SAT   SUN

MEDITATED FOR FULL 15-20 MINUTES

_____: ____/7 =

MON   TUES   WED   THURS   FRI   SAT   SUN

CONSUMED POSITIVE MEDIA FOR FULL 30+ MINUTES

_____: ____/7 =

MON   TUES   WED   THURS   FRI   SAT   SUN

COMPLETED NIGHTLY SELF-CARE

_____: ____/7 =

MON   TUES   WED   THURS   FRI   SAT   SUN

WEEKLY SCORE CARD

WHAT HELPED YOU ACHIEVE 100% ON ALL SELF-LOVE
INVESTMENTS, AND IF YOU DIDN'T, WHAT DO YOU
BELIEVE HINDERED YOU?

_____

_____

WHAT WILL YOU DO TO ACHIEVE 100% NEXT WEEK?

_____

_____

MAJOR TAKEAWAY FROM THIS PAST WEEK THAT YOU'VE
LEARNED ABOUT YOURSELF OR LIFE IN GENERAL?

_____

_____

ONE THING THAT HELPS YOU FEEL YOUR ABSOLUTE BEST
THIS PAST WEEK:

_____

_____

ONE THING THAT MADE YOU FEEL NOT SO GREAT THIS
PAST WEEK:

_____

_____

NAME A WAY YOU WILL CONQUER THAT THING THAT
PREVENTED YOU FROM FEELING YOUR BEST.

_____

_____

WEEK 4

MONDAY

TODAY'S AFFIRMATION:

_____

_____

THREE THINGS YOU ARE GRATEFUL FOR AND WHY:

_____

_____

_____

ONE GOAL YOU'D LIKE TO ACCOMPLISH TODAY
(EMOTIONAL OR MENTAL STATE):

_____

_____

Spend 15-20 minutes in meditation on the things you just wrote.
Initial here when you're done. _____

Spend at least 30 minutes consuming positive media (inspirational podcasts,
books, videos, etc.). *Initial here when you're done.* _____

NIGHTLY SELF-CARE INVESTMENT

Describe an instance where someone or something attempted to take control
of your energy and you did ***not*** allow it. etc.).
Initial here when you're done. _____

ONE THING YOU'RE PROUD OF YOURSELF FOR DOING TODAY IS:

_____

NOTE: Shut down all social media, TVs, and Netflix at least two hours before bed.
Your mind being able to slow down before you go to sleep is critical to its ability to
effectively recharge and handle the tasks of the next day.

TODAY'S AFFIRMATION:

_____

_____

THREE THINGS YOU ARE GRATEFUL FOR AND WHY:

_____

_____

_____

ONE GOAL YOU'D LIKE TO ACCOMPLISH TODAY
(EMOTIONAL OR MENTAL STATE):

_____

_____

Spend 15-20 minutes in meditation on the things you just wrote.
Initial here when you're done. _____

Spend at least 30 minutes consuming positive media (inspirational podcasts, books, videos, etc.). *Initial here when you're done.* _____

NIGHTLY SELF-CARE INVESTMENT

Describe an instance where someone or something attempted to take control of your energy and you did *not* allow it. etc.).
Initial here when you're done. _____

ONE THING YOU'RE PROUD OF YOURSELF FOR DOING TODAY IS:

_____

NOTE: Shut down all social media, TVs, and Netflix at least two hours before bed. Your mind being able to slow down before you go to sleep is critical to its ability to effectively recharge and handle the tasks of the next day.

WEDNESDAY

TODAY'S AFFIRMATION:

_____

_____

THREE THINGS YOU ARE GRATEFUL FOR AND WHY:

_____

_____

_____

ONE GOAL YOU'D LIKE TO ACCOMPLISH TODAY
(EMOTIONAL OR MENTAL STATE):

_____

_____

Spend 15-20 minutes in meditation on the things you just wrote.
Initial here when you're done. _____

Spend at least 30 minutes consuming positive media (inspirational podcasts,
books, videos, etc.). _Initial here when you're done._ _____

NIGHTLY SELF-CARE INVESTMENT

Describe an instance where someone or something attempted to take control
of your energy and you did **_not_** allow it. etc.).
Initial here when you're done. _____

ONE THING YOU'RE PROUD OF YOURSELF FOR DOING TODAY IS:

_____

NOTE: Shut down all social media, TVs, and Netflix at least two hours before bed.
Your mind being able to slow down before you go to sleep is critical to its ability to
effectively recharge and handle the tasks of the next day.

TODAY'S AFFIRMATION:

_____

_____

THREE THINGS YOU ARE GRATEFUL FOR AND WHY:

_____

_____

_____

ONE GOAL YOU'D LIKE TO ACCOMPLISH TODAY
(EMOTIONAL OR MENTAL STATE):

_____

_____

Spend 15-20 minutes in meditation on the things you just wrote.
Initial here when you're done. _____

Spend at least 30 minutes consuming positive media (inspirational podcasts,
books, videos, etc.). *Initial here when you're done.* _____

NIGHTLY SELF-CARE INVESTMENT

Describe an instance where someone or something attempted to take control
of your energy and you did *not* allow it. etc.).
Initial here when you're done. _____

ONE THING YOU'RE PROUD OF YOURSELF FOR DOING TODAY IS:

_____

NOTE: Shut down all social media, TVs, and Netflix at least two hours before bed.
Your mind being able to slow down before you go to sleep is critical to its ability to
effectively recharge and handle the tasks of the next day.

FRIDAY

TODAY'S AFFIRMATION:

_____

_____

THREE THINGS YOU ARE GRATEFUL FOR AND WHY:

_____

_____

_____

ONE GOAL YOU'D LIKE TO ACCOMPLISH TODAY
(EMOTIONAL OR MENTAL STATE):

_____

_____

Spend 15-20 minutes in meditation on the things you just wrote.
Initial here when you're done. _____

Spend at least 30 minutes consuming positive media (inspirational podcasts,
books, videos, etc.). _Initial here when you're done._ _____

NIGHTLY SELF-CARE INVESTMENT

Describe an instance where someone or something attempted to take control
of your energy and you did **not** allow it. etc.).
Initial here when you're done. _____

ONE THING YOU'RE PROUD OF YOURSELF FOR DOING TODAY IS:

_____

NOTE: Shut down all social media, TVs, and Netflix at least two hours before bed.
Your mind being able to slow down before you go to sleep is critical to its ability to
effectively recharge and handle the tasks of the next day.

TODAY'S AFFIRMATION:

_____

_____

THREE THINGS YOU ARE GRATEFUL FOR AND WHY:

_____

_____

_____

ONE GOAL YOU'D LIKE TO ACCOMPLISH TODAY
(EMOTIONAL OR MENTAL STATE):

_____

_____

Spend 15-20 minutes in meditation on the things you just wrote.
Initial here when you're done. _____

Spend at least 30 minutes consuming positive media (inspirational podcasts,
books, videos, etc.). *Initial here when you're done.* _____

NIGHTLY SELF-CARE INVESTMENT

Describe an instance where someone or something attempted to take control
of your energy and you did *not* allow it. etc.).
Initial here when you're done. _____

ONE THING YOU'RE PROUD OF YOURSELF FOR DOING TODAY IS:

_____

NOTE: Shut down all social media, TVs, and Netflix at least two hours before bed.
Your mind being able to slow down before you go to sleep is critical to its ability to
effectively recharge and handle the tasks of the next day.

SUNDAY

TODAY'S AFFIRMATION:

TODAY'S AFFIRMATION:

_____

_____

THREE THINGS YOU ARE GRATEFUL FOR AND WHY:

_____

_____

_____

ONE GOAL YOU'D LIKE TO ACCOMPLISH TODAY
(EMOTIONAL OR MENTAL STATE):

_____

_____

Spend 15-20 minutes in meditation on the things you just wrote.
Initial here when you're done. _____

Spend at least 30 minutes consuming positive media (inspirational podcasts,
books, videos, etc.). _Initial here when you're done._ _____

NIGHTLY SELF-CARE INVESTMENT

Describe an instance where someone or something attempted to take control
of your energy and you did **not** allow it. etc.).
Initial here when you're done. _____

ONE THING YOU'RE PROUD OF YOURSELF FOR DOING TODAY IS:

_____

NOTE: Shut down all social media, TVs, and Netflix at least two hours before bed.
Your mind being able to slow down before you go to sleep is critical to its ability to
effectively recharge and handle the tasks of the next day.

WEEKLY SCORE CARD

WROTE DOWN AFFIRMATION

_____: ____/7 =

MON   TUES   WED   THURS   FRI   SAT   SUN

WROTE DOWN GOALS

_____: ____/7 =

MON   TUES   WED   THURS   FRI   SAT   SUN

MEDITATED FOR FULL 15-20 MINUTES

_____: ____/7 =

MON   TUES   WED   THURS   FRI   SAT   SUN

CONSUMED POSITIVE MEDIA FOR FULL 30+ MINUTES

_____: ____/7 =

MON   TUES   WED   THURS   FRI   SAT   SUN

COMPLETED NIGHTLY SELF-CARE

_____: ____/7 =

MON   TUES   WED   THURS   FRI   SAT   SUN

WEEKLY SCORE CARD

WHAT HELPED YOU ACHIEVE 100% ON ALL SELF-LOVE INVESTMENTS, AND IF YOU DIDN'T, WHAT DO YOU BELIEVE HINDERED YOU?

_____

_____

WHAT WILL YOU DO TO ACHIEVE 100% NEXT WEEK?

_____

_____

MAJOR TAKEAWAY FROM THIS PAST WEEK THAT YOU'VE LEARNED ABOUT YOURSELF OR LIFE IN GENERAL?

_____

_____

ONE THING THAT HELPS YOU FEEL YOUR ABSOLUTE BEST THIS PAST WEEK:

_____

_____

ONE THING THAT MADE YOU FEEL NOT SO GREAT THIS PAST WEEK:

_____

_____

NAME A WAY YOU WILL CONQUER THAT THING THAT PREVENTED YOU FROM FEELING YOUR BEST.

_____

_____

WEEK 5

MONDAY

TODAY'S AFFIRMATION:

_____

_____

THREE THINGS YOU ARE GRATEFUL FOR AND WHY:

_____

_____

_____

ONE GOAL YOU'D LIKE TO ACCOMPLISH TODAY
(EMOTIONAL OR MENTAL STATE):

_____

_____

Spend 15-20 minutes in meditation on the things you just wrote.
Initial here when you're done. _____

Spend at least 30 minutes consuming positive media (inspirational podcasts,
books, videos, etc.). _Initial here when you're done._ _____

NIGHTLY SELF-CARE INVESTMENT

Describe an instance where someone or something attempted to take control
of your energy and you did _not_ allow it. etc.).
Initial here when you're done. _____

ONE THING YOU'RE PROUD OF YOURSELF FOR DOING TODAY IS:

_____

NOTE: Shut down all social media, TVs, and Netflix at least two hours before bed.
Your mind being able to slow down before you go to sleep is critical to its ability to
effectively recharge and handle the tasks of the next day.

TODAY'S AFFIRMATION:

_____

_____

THREE THINGS YOU ARE GRATEFUL FOR AND WHY:

_____

_____

_____

ONE GOAL YOU'D LIKE TO ACCOMPLISH TODAY
(EMOTIONAL OR MENTAL STATE):

_____

_____

Spend 15-20 minutes in meditation on the things you just wrote.
Initial here when you're done. _____

Spend at least 30 minutes consuming positive media (inspirational podcasts, books, videos, etc.). *Initial here when you're done.* _____

NIGHTLY SELF-CARE INVESTMENT

Describe an instance where someone or something attempted to take control of your energy and you did *not* allow it. etc.).
Initial here when you're done. _____

ONE THING YOU'RE PROUD OF YOURSELF FOR DOING TODAY IS:

_____

NOTE: Shut down all social media, TVs, and Netflix at least two hours before bed. Your mind being able to slow down before you go to sleep is critical to its ability to effectively recharge and handle the tasks of the next day.

WEDNESDAY

TODAY'S AFFIRMATION:

_____

_____

THREE THINGS YOU ARE GRATEFUL FOR AND WHY:

_____

_____

_____

ONE GOAL YOU'D LIKE TO ACCOMPLISH TODAY
(EMOTIONAL OR MENTAL STATE):

_____

_____

Spend 15-20 minutes in meditation on the things you just wrote.
Initial here when you're done. _____

Spend at least 30 minutes consuming positive media (inspirational podcasts,
books, videos, etc.). *Initial here when you're done.* _____

NIGHTLY SELF-CARE INVESTMENT

Describe an instance where someone or something attempted to take control
of your energy and you did *not* allow it. etc.).
Initial here when you're done. _____

ONE THING YOU'RE PROUD OF YOURSELF FOR DOING TODAY IS:

_____

NOTE: Shut down all social media, TVs, and Netflix at least two hours before bed.
Your mind being able to slow down before you go to sleep is critical to its ability to
effectively recharge and handle the tasks of the next day.

THURSDAY

TODAY'S AFFIRMATION:

_____

_____

THREE THINGS YOU ARE GRATEFUL FOR AND WHY:

_____

_____

_____

ONE GOAL YOU'D LIKE TO ACCOMPLISH TODAY
(EMOTIONAL OR MENTAL STATE):

_____

_____

Spend 15-20 minutes in meditation on the things you just wrote.
Initial here when you're done. _____

Spend at least 30 minutes consuming positive media (inspirational podcasts,
books, videos, etc.). _Initial here when you're done._ _____

NIGHTLY SELF-CARE INVESTMENT

Describe an instance where someone or something attempted to take control
of your energy and you did _not_ allow it. etc.).
Initial here when you're done. _____

ONE THING YOU'RE PROUD OF YOURSELF FOR DOING TODAY IS:

_____

NOTE: Shut down all social media, TVs, and Netflix at least two hours before bed.
Your mind being able to slow down before you go to sleep is critical to its ability to
effectively recharge and handle the tasks of the next day.

FRIDAY

TODAY'S AFFIRMATION:

_____

_____

THREE THINGS YOU ARE GRATEFUL FOR AND WHY:

_____

_____

_____

ONE GOAL YOU'D LIKE TO ACCOMPLISH TODAY
(EMOTIONAL OR MENTAL STATE):

_____

_____

Spend 15-20 minutes in meditation on the things you just wrote.
Initial here when you're done. _____

Spend at least 30 minutes consuming positive media (inspirational podcasts,
books, videos, etc.). _Initial here when you're done._ _____

NIGHTLY SELF-CARE INVESTMENT

**Describe an instance where someone or something attempted to take control
of your energy and you did _not_ allow it. etc.).**
Initial here when you're done. _____

ONE THING YOU'RE PROUD OF YOURSELF FOR DOING TODAY IS:

_____

NOTE: Shut down all social media, TVs, and Netflix at least two hours before bed.
Your mind being able to slow down before you go to sleep is critical to its ability to
effectively recharge and handle the tasks of the next day.

TODAY'S AFFIRMATION:

_____

_____

THREE THINGS YOU ARE GRATEFUL FOR AND WHY:

_____

_____

_____

ONE GOAL YOU'D LIKE TO ACCOMPLISH TODAY
(EMOTIONAL OR MENTAL STATE):

_____

_____

Spend 15-20 minutes in meditation on the things you just wrote.
Initial here when you're done. _____

Spend at least 30 minutes consuming positive media (inspirational podcasts, books, videos, etc.). _Initial here when you're done._ _____

⚜ NIGHTLY SELF-CARE INVESTMENT

Describe an instance where someone or something attempted to take control of your energy and you did _not_ allow it. etc.).
Initial here when you're done. _____

ONE THING YOU'RE PROUD OF YOURSELF FOR DOING TODAY IS:

_____

NOTE: Shut down all social media, TVs, and Netflix at least two hours before bed. Your mind being able to slow down before you go to sleep is critical to its ability to effectively recharge and handle the tasks of the next day.

SUNDAY

TODAY'S AFFIRMATION:

_____

_____

THREE THINGS YOU ARE GRATEFUL FOR AND WHY:

_____

_____

_____

ONE GOAL YOU'D LIKE TO ACCOMPLISH TODAY
(EMOTIONAL OR MENTAL STATE):

_____

_____

Spend 15-20 minutes in meditation on the things you just wrote.
Initial here when you're done. _____

Spend at least 30 minutes consuming positive media (inspirational podcasts,
books, videos, etc.). _Initial here when you're done._ _____

NIGHTLY SELF-CARE INVESTMENT

Describe an instance where someone or something attempted to take control
of your energy and you did _not_ allow it. etc.).
Initial here when you're done. _____

ONE THING YOU'RE PROUD OF YOURSELF FOR DOING TODAY IS:

_____

NOTE: Shut down all social media, TVs, and Netflix at least two hours before bed.
Your mind being able to slow down before you go to sleep is critical to its ability to
effectively recharge and handle the tasks of the next day.

WEEKLY SCORE CARD

WROTE DOWN AFFIRMATION

_____: ____/7 =

MON   TUES   WED   THURS   FRI   SAT   SUN

WROTE DOWN GOALS

_____: ____/7 =

MON   TUES   WED   THURS   FRI   SAT   SUN

MEDITATED FOR FULL 15-20 MINUTES

_____: ____/7 =

MON   TUES   WED   THURS   FRI   SAT   SUN

CONSUMED POSITIVE MEDIA FOR FULL 30+ MINUTES

_____: ____/7 =

MON   TUES   WED   THURS   FRI   SAT   SUN

COMPLETED NIGHTLY SELF-CARE

_____: ____/7 =

MON   TUES   WED   THURS   FRI   SAT   SUN

WEEKLY SCORE CARD

WHAT HELPED YOU ACHIEVE 100% ON ALL SELF-LOVE
INVESTMENTS, AND IF YOU DIDN'T, WHAT DO YOU
BELIEVE HINDERED YOU?

_____

_____

WHAT WILL YOU DO TO ACHIEVE 100% NEXT WEEK?

_____

_____

MAJOR TAKEAWAY FROM THIS PAST WEEK THAT YOU'VE
LEARNED ABOUT YOURSELF OR LIFE IN GENERAL?

_____

_____

ONE THING THAT HELPS YOU FEEL YOUR ABSOLUTE BEST
THIS PAST WEEK:

_____

_____

ONE THING THAT MADE YOU FEEL NOT SO GREAT THIS
PAST WEEK:

_____

_____

NAME A WAY YOU WILL CONQUER THAT THING THAT
PREVENTED YOU FROM FEELING YOUR BEST.

_____

_____

WEEK 6

MONDAY

TODAY'S AFFIRMATION:

_____

_____

THREE THINGS YOU ARE GRATEFUL FOR AND WHY:

_____

_____

_____

ONE GOAL YOU'D LIKE TO ACCOMPLISH TODAY
(EMOTIONAL OR MENTAL STATE):

_____

_____

Spend 15-20 minutes in meditation on the things you just wrote.
Initial here when you're done. _____

Spend at least 30 minutes consuming positive media (inspirational podcasts,
books, videos, etc.). *Initial here when you're done.* _____

⚜ NIGHTLY SELF-CARE INVESTMENT

Describe an instance where someone or something attempted to take control
of your energy and you did *not* allow it. etc.).
Initial here when you're done. _____

ONE THING YOU'RE PROUD OF YOURSELF FOR DOING TODAY IS:

_____

NOTE: Shut down all social media, TVs, and Netflix at least two hours before bed.
Your mind being able to slow down before you go to sleep is critical to its ability to
effectively recharge and handle the tasks of the next day.

TODAY'S AFFIRMATION:

_____

_____

THREE THINGS YOU ARE GRATEFUL FOR AND WHY:

_____

_____

_____

ONE GOAL YOU'D LIKE TO ACCOMPLISH TODAY
(EMOTIONAL OR MENTAL STATE):

_____

_____

Spend 15-20 minutes in meditation on the things you just wrote.
Initial here when you're done. _____

Spend at least 30 minutes consuming positive media (inspirational podcasts,
books, videos, etc.). *Initial here when you're done.* _____

NIGHTLY SELF-CARE INVESTMENT

Describe an instance where someone or something attempted to take control
of your energy and you did *not* allow it. etc.).
Initial here when you're done. _____

ONE THING YOU'RE PROUD OF YOURSELF FOR DOING TODAY IS:

_____

NOTE: Shut down all social media, TVs, and Netflix at least two hours before bed.
Your mind being able to slow down before you go to sleep is critical to its ability to
effectively recharge and handle the tasks of the next day.

WEDNESDAY

TODAY'S AFFIRMATION:

_____

_____

THREE THINGS YOU ARE GRATEFUL FOR AND WHY:

_____

_____

_____

ONE GOAL YOU'D LIKE TO ACCOMPLISH TODAY
(EMOTIONAL OR MENTAL STATE):

_____

_____

Spend 15-20 minutes in meditation on the things you just wrote.
Initial here when you're done. _____

Spend at least 30 minutes consuming positive media (inspirational podcasts,
books, videos, etc.). _Initial here when you're done._ _____

NIGHTLY SELF-CARE INVESTMENT

Describe an instance where someone or something attempted to take control
of your energy and you did **not** allow it. etc.).
Initial here when you're done. _____

ONE THING YOU'RE PROUD OF YOURSELF FOR DOING TODAY IS:

_____

NOTE: Shut down all social media, TVs, and Netflix at least two hours before bed.
Your mind being able to slow down before you go to sleep is critical to its ability to
effectively recharge and handle the tasks of the next day.

TODAY'S AFFIRMATION:

_____

_____

THREE THINGS YOU ARE GRATEFUL FOR AND WHY:

_____

_____

_____

ONE GOAL YOU'D LIKE TO ACCOMPLISH TODAY
(EMOTIONAL OR MENTAL STATE):

_____

_____

Spend 15-20 minutes in meditation on the things you just wrote.
Initial here when you're done. _____

Spend at least 30 minutes consuming positive media (inspirational podcasts, books, videos, etc.). *Initial here when you're done.* _____

♛ NIGHTLY SELF-CARE INVESTMENT

Describe an instance where someone or something attempted to take control of your energy and you did *not* allow it. etc.).
Initial here when you're done. _____

ONE THING YOU'RE PROUD OF YOURSELF FOR DOING TODAY IS:

_____

NOTE: Shut down all social media, TVs, and Netflix at least two hours before bed. Your mind being able to slow down before you go to sleep is critical to its ability to effectively recharge and handle the tasks of the next day.

FRIDAY

TODAY'S AFFIRMATION:

_____

_____

THREE THINGS YOU ARE GRATEFUL FOR AND WHY:

_____

_____

_____

ONE GOAL YOU'D LIKE TO ACCOMPLISH TODAY
(EMOTIONAL OR MENTAL STATE):

_____

_____

Spend 15-20 minutes in meditation on the things you just wrote.
Initial here when you're done. _____

Spend at least 30 minutes consuming positive media (inspirational podcasts, books, videos, etc.). _Initial here when you're done._ _____

NIGHTLY SELF-CARE INVESTMENT

Describe an instance where someone or something attempted to take control of your energy and you did _not_ allow it. etc.).
Initial here when you're done. _____

ONE THING YOU'RE PROUD OF YOURSELF FOR DOING TODAY IS:

_____

NOTE: Shut down all social media, TVs, and Netflix at least two hours before bed. Your mind being able to slow down before you go to sleep is critical to its ability to effectively recharge and handle the tasks of the next day.

SATURDAY

TODAY'S AFFIRMATION:

_____

_____

THREE THINGS YOU ARE GRATEFUL FOR AND WHY:

_____

_____

_____

ONE GOAL YOU'D LIKE TO ACCOMPLISH TODAY
(EMOTIONAL OR MENTAL STATE):

_____

_____

Spend 15-20 minutes in meditation on the things you just wrote.
Initial here when you're done. _____

Spend at least 30 minutes consuming positive media (inspirational podcasts,
books, videos, etc.). _Initial here when you're done._ _____

NIGHTLY SELF-CARE INVESTMENT

Describe an instance where someone or something attempted to take control
of your energy and you did **not** allow it. etc.).
Initial here when you're done. _____

ONE THING YOU'RE PROUD OF YOURSELF FOR DOING TODAY IS:

_____

NOTE: Shut down all social media, TVs, and Netflix at least two hours before bed.
Your mind being able to slow down before you go to sleep is critical to its ability to
effectively recharge and handle the tasks of the next day.

SUNDAY

TODAY'S AFFIRMATION:

_____

_____

THREE THINGS YOU ARE GRATEFUL FOR AND WHY:

_____

_____

_____

ONE GOAL YOU'D LIKE TO ACCOMPLISH TODAY
(EMOTIONAL OR MENTAL STATE):

_____

_____

Spend 15-20 minutes in meditation on the things you just wrote.
Initial here when you're done. _____

Spend at least 30 minutes consuming positive media (inspirational podcasts,
books, videos, etc.). _Initial here when you're done._ _____

NIGHTLY SELF-CARE INVESTMENT

Describe an instance where someone or something attempted to take control
of your energy and you did _**not**_ allow it. etc.).
Initial here when you're done. _____

ONE THING YOU'RE PROUD OF YOURSELF FOR DOING TODAY IS:

_____

NOTE: Shut down all social media, TVs, and Netflix at least two hours before bed.
Your mind being able to slow down before you go to sleep is critical to its ability to
effectively recharge and handle the tasks of the next day.

WEEKLY SCORE CARD

WROTE DOWN AFFIRMATION

_____: ____/7 =

MON   TUES   WED   THURS   FRI   SAT   SUN

WROTE DOWN GOALS

_____: ____/7 =

MON   TUES   WED   THURS   FRI   SAT   SUN

MEDITATED FOR FULL 15-20 MINUTES

_____: ____/7 =

MON   TUES   WED   THURS   FRI   SAT   SUN

CONSUMED POSITIVE MEDIA FOR FULL 30+ MINUTES

_____: ____/7 =

MON   TUES   WED   THURS   FRI   SAT   SUN

COMPLETED NIGHTLY SELF-CARE

_____: ____/7 =

MON   TUES   WED   THURS   FRI   SAT   SUN

WEEKLY SCORE CARD

WHAT HELPED YOU ACHIEVE 100% ON ALL SELF-LOVE
INVESTMENTS, AND IF YOU DIDN'T, WHAT DO YOU
BELIEVE HINDERED YOU?

_____

_____

WHAT WILL YOU DO TO ACHIEVE 100% NEXT WEEK?

_____

_____

MAJOR TAKEAWAY FROM THIS PAST WEEK THAT YOU'VE
LEARNED ABOUT YOURSELF OR LIFE IN GENERAL?

_____

_____

ONE THING THAT HELPS YOU FEEL YOUR ABSOLUTE BEST
THIS PAST WEEK:

_____

_____

ONE THING THAT MADE YOU FEEL NOT SO GREAT THIS
PAST WEEK:

_____

_____

NAME A WAY YOU WILL CONQUER THAT THING THAT
PREVENTED YOU FROM FEELING YOUR BEST.

_____

_____

WEEK 7

MONDAY

TODAY'S AFFIRMATION:

_____

_____

THREE THINGS YOU ARE GRATEFUL FOR AND WHY:

_____

_____

_____

ONE GOAL YOU'D LIKE TO ACCOMPLISH TODAY
(EMOTIONAL OR MENTAL STATE):

_____

_____

Spend 15-20 minutes in meditation on the things you just wrote.
Initial here when you're done. _____

Spend at least 30 minutes consuming positive media (inspirational podcasts,
books, videos, etc.). _Initial here when you're done._ _____

NIGHTLY SELF-CARE INVESTMENT

Describe an instance where someone or something attempted to take control
of your energy and you did _**not**_ allow it. etc.).
Initial here when you're done. _____

ONE THING YOU'RE PROUD OF YOURSELF FOR DOING TODAY IS:

_____

NOTE: Shut down all social media, TVs, and Netflix at least two hours before bed.
Your mind being able to slow down before you go to sleep is critical to its ability to
effectively recharge and handle the tasks of the next day.

TODAY'S AFFIRMATION:

_____

_____

THREE THINGS YOU ARE GRATEFUL FOR AND WHY:

_____

_____

_____

ONE GOAL YOU'D LIKE TO ACCOMPLISH TODAY
(EMOTIONAL OR MENTAL STATE):

_____

_____

Spend 15-20 minutes in meditation on the things you just wrote.
Initial here when you're done. _____

Spend at least 30 minutes consuming positive media (inspirational podcasts, books, videos, etc.). _Initial here when you're done._ _____

NIGHTLY SELF-CARE INVESTMENT

Describe an instance where someone or something attempted to take control of your energy and you did _not_ allow it. etc.).
Initial here when you're done. _____

ONE THING YOU'RE PROUD OF YOURSELF FOR DOING TODAY IS:

_____

NOTE: Shut down all social media, TVs, and Netflix at least two hours before bed. Your mind being able to slow down before you go to sleep is critical to its ability to effectively recharge and handle the tasks of the next day.

WEDNESDAY

TODAY'S AFFIRMATION:

_____

_____

THREE THINGS YOU ARE GRATEFUL FOR AND WHY:

_____

_____

_____

ONE GOAL YOU'D LIKE TO ACCOMPLISH TODAY
(EMOTIONAL OR MENTAL STATE):

_____

_____

Spend 15-20 minutes in meditation on the things you just wrote.
Initial here when you're done. _____

Spend at least 30 minutes consuming positive media (inspirational podcasts, books, videos, etc.). _Initial here when you're done._ _____

NIGHTLY SELF-CARE INVESTMENT

Describe an instance where someone or something attempted to take control of your energy and you did _not_ allow it. etc.).
Initial here when you're done. _____

ONE THING YOU'RE PROUD OF YOURSELF FOR DOING TODAY IS:

_____

NOTE: Shut down all social media, TVs, and Netflix at least two hours before bed. Your mind being able to slow down before you go to sleep is critical to its ability to effectively recharge and handle the tasks of the next day.

TODAY'S AFFIRMATION:

_____

_____

THREE THINGS YOU ARE GRATEFUL FOR AND WHY:

_____

_____

_____

ONE GOAL YOU'D LIKE TO ACCOMPLISH TODAY
(EMOTIONAL OR MENTAL STATE):

_____

_____

Spend 15-20 minutes in meditation on the things you just wrote.
Initial here when you're done. _____

Spend at least 30 minutes consuming positive media (inspirational podcasts, books, videos, etc.). *Initial here when you're done.* _____

♕ NIGHTLY SELF-CARE INVESTMENT

Describe an instance where someone or something attempted to take control of your energy and you did **not** allow it. etc.).
Initial here when you're done. _____

ONE THING YOU'RE PROUD OF YOURSELF FOR DOING TODAY IS:

_____

NOTE: Shut down all social media, TVs, and Netflix at least two hours before bed. Your mind being able to slow down before you go to sleep is critical to its ability to effectively recharge and handle the tasks of the next day.

FRIDAY

TODAY'S AFFIRMATION:

_____

_____

THREE THINGS YOU ARE GRATEFUL FOR AND WHY:

_____

_____

_____

ONE GOAL YOU'D LIKE TO ACCOMPLISH TODAY
(EMOTIONAL OR MENTAL STATE):

_____

_____

Spend 15-20 minutes in meditation on the things you just wrote.
Initial here when you're done. _____

Spend at least 30 minutes consuming positive media (inspirational podcasts,
books, videos, etc.). *Initial here when you're done.* _____

NIGHTLY SELF-CARE INVESTMENT

Describe an instance where someone or something attempted to take control
of your energy and you did ***not*** allow it. etc.).
Initial here when you're done. _____

ONE THING YOU'RE PROUD OF YOURSELF FOR DOING TODAY IS:

_____

NOTE: Shut down all social media, TVs, and Netflix at least two hours before bed.
Your mind being able to slow down before you go to sleep is critical to its ability to
effectively recharge and handle the tasks of the next day.

TODAY'S AFFIRMATION:

_____

_____

THREE THINGS YOU ARE GRATEFUL FOR AND WHY:

_____

_____

_____

ONE GOAL YOU'D LIKE TO ACCOMPLISH TODAY
(EMOTIONAL OR MENTAL STATE):

_____

_____

Spend 15-20 minutes in meditation on the things you just wrote.
Initial here when you're done. _____

Spend at least 30 minutes consuming positive media (inspirational podcasts, books, videos, etc.). *Initial here when you're done.* _____

👑 NIGHTLY SELF-CARE INVESTMENT

Describe an instance where someone or something attempted to take control of your energy and you did *not* allow it. etc.).
Initial here when you're done. _____

ONE THING YOU'RE PROUD OF YOURSELF FOR DOING TODAY IS:

_____

NOTE: Shut down all social media, TVs, and Netflix at least two hours before bed. Your mind being able to slow down before you go to sleep is critical to its ability to effectively recharge and handle the tasks of the next day.

SUNDAY

TODAY'S AFFIRMATION:

_____

_____

THREE THINGS YOU ARE GRATEFUL FOR AND WHY:

_____

_____

_____

ONE GOAL YOU'D LIKE TO ACCOMPLISH TODAY
(EMOTIONAL OR MENTAL STATE):

_____

_____

Spend 15-20 minutes in meditation on the things you just wrote.
Initial here when you're done. _____

Spend at least 30 minutes consuming positive media (inspirational podcasts, books, videos, etc.). _Initial here when you're done._ _____

NIGHTLY SELF-CARE INVESTMENT

Describe an instance where someone or something attempted to take control of your energy and you did _**not**_ allow it. etc.).
Initial here when you're done. _____

ONE THING YOU'RE PROUD OF YOURSELF FOR DOING TODAY IS:

_____

NOTE: Shut down all social media, TVs, and Netflix at least two hours before bed. Your mind being able to slow down before you go to sleep is critical to its ability to effectively recharge and handle the tasks of the next day.

WEEKLY SCORE CARD

WROTE DOWN AFFIRMATION

_____: ____/7 =

MON   TUES   WED   THURS   FRI   SAT   SUN

WROTE DOWN GOALS

_____: ____/7 =

MON   TUES   WED   THURS   FRI   SAT   SUN

MEDITATED FOR FULL 15-20 MINUTES

_____: ____/7 =

MON   TUES   WED   THURS   FRI   SAT   SUN

CONSUMED POSITIVE MEDIA FOR FULL 30+ MINUTES

_____: ____/7 =

MON   TUES   WED   THURS   FRI   SAT   SUN

COMPLETED NIGHTLY SELF-CARE

_____: ____/7 =

MON   TUES   WED   THURS   FRI   SAT   SUN

WEEKLY SCORE CARD

WHAT HELPED YOU ACHIEVE 100% ON ALL SELF-LOVE
INVESTMENTS, AND IF YOU DIDN'T, WHAT DO YOU
BELIEVE HINDERED YOU?

_____

_____

WHAT WILL YOU DO TO ACHIEVE 100% NEXT WEEK?

_____

_____

MAJOR TAKEAWAY FROM THIS PAST WEEK THAT YOU'VE
LEARNED ABOUT YOURSELF OR LIFE IN GENERAL?

_____

_____

ONE THING THAT HELPS YOU FEEL YOUR ABSOLUTE BEST
THIS PAST WEEK:

_____

_____

ONE THING THAT MADE YOU FEEL NOT SO GREAT THIS
PAST WEEK:

_____

_____

NAME A WAY YOU WILL CONQUER THAT THING THAT
PREVENTED YOU FROM FEELING YOUR BEST.

_____

_____

WEEK 8

MONDAY

TODAY'S AFFIRMATION:

_____

_____

THREE THINGS YOU ARE GRATEFUL FOR AND WHY:

_____

_____

_____

ONE GOAL YOU'D LIKE TO ACCOMPLISH TODAY
(EMOTIONAL OR MENTAL STATE):

_____

_____

Spend 15-20 minutes in meditation on the things you just wrote.
Initial here when you're done. _____

Spend at least 30 minutes consuming positive media (inspirational podcasts,
books, videos, etc.). _Initial here when you're done._ _____

NIGHTLY SELF-CARE INVESTMENT

Describe an instance where someone or something attempted to take control
of your energy and you did **not** allow it. etc.).
Initial here when you're done. _____

ONE THING YOU'RE PROUD OF YOURSELF FOR DOING TODAY IS:

_____

NOTE: Shut down all social media, TVs, and Netflix at least two hours before bed.
Your mind being able to slow down before you go to sleep is critical to its ability to
effectively recharge and handle the tasks of the next day.

TODAY'S AFFIRMATION:

_____

_____

THREE THINGS YOU ARE GRATEFUL FOR AND WHY:

_____

_____

_____

ONE GOAL YOU'D LIKE TO ACCOMPLISH TODAY
(EMOTIONAL OR MENTAL STATE):

_____

_____

Spend 15-20 minutes in meditation on the things you just wrote.
Initial here when you're done. _____

Spend at least 30 minutes consuming positive media (inspirational podcasts,
books, videos, etc.). *Initial here when you're done.* _____

NIGHTLY SELF-CARE INVESTMENT

Describe an instance where someone or something attempted to take control
of your energy and you did *not* allow it. etc.).
Initial here when you're done. _____

ONE THING YOU'RE PROUD OF YOURSELF FOR DOING TODAY IS:

_____

NOTE: Shut down all social media, TVs, and Netflix at least two hours before bed.
Your mind being able to slow down before you go to sleep is critical to its ability to
effectively recharge and handle the tasks of the next day.

WEDNESDAY

TODAY'S AFFIRMATION:

_____

_____

THREE THINGS YOU ARE GRATEFUL FOR AND WHY:

_____

_____

_____

ONE GOAL YOU'D LIKE TO ACCOMPLISH TODAY
(EMOTIONAL OR MENTAL STATE):

_____

_____

Spend 15-20 minutes in meditation on the things you just wrote.
Initial here when you're done. _____

Spend at least 30 minutes consuming positive media (inspirational podcasts,
books, videos, etc.). _Initial here when you're done._ _____

NIGHTLY SELF-CARE INVESTMENT

Describe an instance where someone or something attempted to take control
of your energy and you did **not** allow it. etc.).
Initial here when you're done. _____

ONE THING YOU'RE PROUD OF YOURSELF FOR DOING TODAY IS:

_____

NOTE: Shut down all social media, TVs, and Netflix at least two hours before bed.
Your mind being able to slow down before you go to sleep is critical to its ability to
effectively recharge and handle the tasks of the next day.

TODAY'S AFFIRMATION:

_____

_____

THREE THINGS YOU ARE GRATEFUL FOR AND WHY:

_____

_____

_____

ONE GOAL YOU'D LIKE TO ACCOMPLISH TODAY
(EMOTIONAL OR MENTAL STATE):

_____

_____

Spend 15-20 minutes in meditation on the things you just wrote.
Initial here when you're done. _____

Spend at least 30 minutes consuming positive media (inspirational podcasts, books, videos, etc.). _Initial here when you're done._ _____

NIGHTLY SELF-CARE INVESTMENT

Describe an instance where someone or something attempted to take control of your energy and you did **not** allow it. etc.).
Initial here when you're done. _____

ONE THING YOU'RE PROUD OF YOURSELF FOR DOING TODAY IS:

_____

NOTE: Shut down all social media, TVs, and Netflix at least two hours before bed. Your mind being able to slow down before you go to sleep is critical to its ability to effectively recharge and handle the tasks of the next day.

FRIDAY

TODAY'S AFFIRMATION:

_____

_____

THREE THINGS YOU ARE GRATEFUL FOR AND WHY:

_____

_____

_____

ONE GOAL YOU'D LIKE TO ACCOMPLISH TODAY
(EMOTIONAL OR MENTAL STATE):

_____

_____

Spend 15-20 minutes in meditation on the things you just wrote.
Initial here when you're done. _____

Spend at least 30 minutes consuming positive media (inspirational podcasts,
books, videos, etc.). _Initial here when you're done._ _____

⚜ NIGHTLY SELF-CARE INVESTMENT

Describe an instance where someone or something attempted to take control
of your energy and you did _not_ allow it. etc.).
Initial here when you're done. _____

ONE THING YOU'RE PROUD OF YOURSELF FOR DOING TODAY IS:

_____

NOTE: Shut down all social media, TVs, and Netflix at least two hours before bed.
Your mind being able to slow down before you go to sleep is critical to its ability to
effectively recharge and handle the tasks of the next day.

TODAY'S AFFIRMATION:

_____

_____

THREE THINGS YOU ARE GRATEFUL FOR AND WHY:

_____

_____

_____

ONE GOAL YOU'D LIKE TO ACCOMPLISH TODAY
(EMOTIONAL OR MENTAL STATE):

_____

_____

Spend 15-20 minutes in meditation on the things you just wrote.
Initial here when you're done. _____

Spend at least 30 minutes consuming positive media (inspirational podcasts,
books, videos, etc.). *Initial here when you're done.* _____

NIGHTLY SELF-CARE INVESTMENT

Describe an instance where someone or something attempted to take control
of your energy and you did *not* allow it. etc.).
Initial here when you're done. _____

ONE THING YOU'RE PROUD OF YOURSELF FOR DOING TODAY IS:

_____

NOTE: Shut down all social media, TVs, and Netflix at least two hours before bed.
Your mind being able to slow down before you go to sleep is critical to its ability to
effectively recharge and handle the tasks of the next day.

SUNDAY

TODAY'S AFFIRMATION:

_____

_____

THREE THINGS YOU ARE GRATEFUL FOR AND WHY:

_____

_____

_____

ONE GOAL YOU'D LIKE TO ACCOMPLISH TODAY
(EMOTIONAL OR MENTAL STATE):

_____

_____

Spend 15-20 minutes in meditation on the things you just wrote.
Initial here when you're done. _____

Spend at least 30 minutes consuming positive media (inspirational podcasts,
books, videos, etc.). _Initial here when you're done._ _____

NIGHTLY SELF-CARE INVESTMENT

Describe an instance where someone or something attempted to take control
of your energy and you did **not** allow it. etc.).
Initial here when you're done. _____

ONE THING YOU'RE PROUD OF YOURSELF FOR DOING TODAY IS:

_____

NOTE: Shut down all social media, TVs, and Netflix at least two hours before bed.
Your mind being able to slow down before you go to sleep is critical to its ability to
effectively recharge and handle the tasks of the next day.

WEEKLY SCORE CARD

WROTE DOWN AFFIRMATION

_____: ____/7 =

MON   TUES   WED   THURS   FRI   SAT   SUN

WROTE DOWN GOALS

_____: ____/7 =

MON   TUES   WED   THURS   FRI   SAT   SUN

MEDITATED FOR FULL 15-20 MINUTES

_____: ____/7 =

MON   TUES   WED   THURS   FRI   SAT   SUN

CONSUMED POSITIVE MEDIA FOR FULL 30+ MINUTES

_____: ____/7 =

MON   TUES   WED   THURS   FRI   SAT   SUN

COMPLETED NIGHTLY SELF-CARE

_____: ____/7 =

MON   TUES   WED   THURS   FRI   SAT   SUN

WEEKLY SCORE CARD

WHAT HELPED YOU ACHIEVE 100% ON ALL SELF-LOVE
INVESTMENTS, AND IF YOU DIDN'T, WHAT DO YOU
BELIEVE HINDERED YOU?

_____

_____

WHAT WILL YOU DO TO ACHIEVE 100% NEXT WEEK?

_____

_____

MAJOR TAKEAWAY FROM THIS PAST WEEK THAT YOU'VE
LEARNED ABOUT YOURSELF OR LIFE IN GENERAL?

_____

_____

ONE THING THAT HELPS YOU FEEL YOUR ABSOLUTE BEST
THIS PAST WEEK:

_____

_____

ONE THING THAT MADE YOU FEEL NOT SO GREAT THIS
PAST WEEK:

_____

_____

NAME A WAY YOU WILL CONQUER THAT THING THAT
PREVENTED YOU FROM FEELING YOUR BEST.

_____

_____

WEEK 9

MONDAY

_____

_____

THREE THINGS YOU ARE GRATEFUL FOR AND WHY:

_____

_____

_____

ONE GOAL YOU'D LIKE TO ACCOMPLISH TODAY
(EMOTIONAL OR MENTAL STATE):

_____

_____

Spend 15-20 minutes in meditation on the things you just wrote.
Initial here when you're done. _____

Spend at least 30 minutes consuming positive media (inspirational podcasts,
books, videos, etc.). _Initial here when you're done._ _____

NIGHTLY SELF-CARE INVESTMENT

Describe an instance where someone or something attempted to take control
of your energy and you did **not** allow it. etc.).
Initial here when you're done. _____

ONE THING YOU'RE PROUD OF YOURSELF FOR DOING TODAY IS:

_____

NOTE: Shut down all social media, TVs, and Netflix at least two hours before bed.
Your mind being able to slow down before you go to sleep is critical to its ability to
effectively recharge and handle the tasks of the next day.

TUESDAY

TODAY'S AFFIRMATION:

_____

_____

THREE THINGS YOU ARE GRATEFUL FOR AND WHY:

_____

_____

_____

ONE GOAL YOU'D LIKE TO ACCOMPLISH TODAY
(EMOTIONAL OR MENTAL STATE):

_____

_____

Spend 15-20 minutes in meditation on the things you just wrote.
Initial here when you're done. _____

Spend at least 30 minutes consuming positive media (inspirational podcasts,
books, videos, etc.). *Initial here when you're done.* _____

NIGHTLY SELF-CARE INVESTMENT

Describe an instance where someone or something attempted to take control
of your energy and you did *not* allow it. etc.).
Initial here when you're done. _____

ONE THING YOU'RE PROUD OF YOURSELF FOR DOING TODAY IS:

_____

NOTE: Shut down all social media, TVs, and Netflix at least two hours before bed.
Your mind being able to slow down before you go to sleep is critical to its ability to
effectively recharge and handle the tasks of the next day.

WEDNESDAY

TODAY'S AFFIRMATION:

_____

_____

THREE THINGS YOU ARE GRATEFUL FOR AND WHY:

_____

_____

_____

ONE GOAL YOU'D LIKE TO ACCOMPLISH TODAY
(EMOTIONAL OR MENTAL STATE):

_____

_____

Spend 15-20 minutes in meditation on the things you just wrote.
Initial here when you're done. _____

Spend at least 30 minutes consuming positive media (inspirational podcasts,
books, videos, etc.). _Initial here when you're done._ _____

NIGHTLY SELF-CARE INVESTMENT

Describe an instance where someone or something attempted to take control
of your energy and you did _not_ allow it. etc.).
Initial here when you're done. _____

ONE THING YOU'RE PROUD OF YOURSELF FOR DOING TODAY IS:

_____

NOTE: Shut down all social media, TVs, and Netflix at least two hours before bed.
Your mind being able to slow down before you go to sleep is critical to its ability to
effectively recharge and handle the tasks of the next day.

TODAY'S AFFIRMATION:

_____

_____

THREE THINGS YOU ARE GRATEFUL FOR AND WHY:

_____

_____

_____

ONE GOAL YOU'D LIKE TO ACCOMPLISH TODAY
(EMOTIONAL OR MENTAL STATE):

_____

_____

Spend 15-20 minutes in meditation on the things you just wrote.
Initial here when you're done. _____

Spend at least 30 minutes consuming positive media (inspirational podcasts,
books, videos, etc.). *Initial here when you're done.* _____

NIGHTLY SELF-CARE INVESTMENT

Describe an instance where someone or something attempted to take control
of your energy and you did *not* allow it. etc.).
Initial here when you're done. _____

ONE THING YOU'RE PROUD OF YOURSELF FOR DOING TODAY IS:

_____

NOTE: Shut down all social media, TVs, and Netflix at least two hours before bed.
Your mind being able to slow down before you go to sleep is critical to its ability to
effectively recharge and handle the tasks of the next day.

FRIDAY

TODAY'S AFFIRMATION:

_____

_____

THREE THINGS YOU ARE GRATEFUL FOR AND WHY:

_____

_____

_____

ONE GOAL YOU'D LIKE TO ACCOMPLISH TODAY
(EMOTIONAL OR MENTAL STATE):

_____

_____

Spend 15-20 minutes in meditation on the things you just wrote.
Initial here when you're done. _____

Spend at least 30 minutes consuming positive media (inspirational podcasts,
books, videos, etc.). _Initial here when you're done._ _____

NIGHTLY SELF-CARE INVESTMENT

Describe an instance where someone or something attempted to take control
of your energy and you did _not_ allow it. etc.).
Initial here when you're done. _____

ONE THING YOU'RE PROUD OF YOURSELF FOR DOING TODAY IS:

_____

NOTE: Shut down all social media, TVs, and Netflix at least two hours before bed.
Your mind being able to slow down before you go to sleep is critical to its ability to
effectively recharge and handle the tasks of the next day.

TODAY'S AFFIRMATION:

_____

_____

THREE THINGS YOU ARE GRATEFUL FOR AND WHY:

_____

_____

_____

ONE GOAL YOU'D LIKE TO ACCOMPLISH TODAY
(EMOTIONAL OR MENTAL STATE):

_____

_____

Spend 15-20 minutes in meditation on the things you just wrote.
Initial here when you're done. _____

Spend at least 30 minutes consuming positive media (inspirational podcasts,
books, videos, etc.). *Initial here when you're done.* _____

NIGHTLY SELF-CARE INVESTMENT

Describe an instance where someone or something attempted to take control
of your energy and you did **not** allow it. etc.).
Initial here when you're done. _____

ONE THING YOU'RE PROUD OF YOURSELF FOR DOING TODAY IS:

_____

NOTE: Shut down all social media, TVs, and Netflix at least two hours before bed.
Your mind being able to slow down before you go to sleep is critical to its ability to
effectively recharge and handle the tasks of the next day.

SUNDAY

TODAY'S AFFIRMATION:

_____

_____

THREE THINGS YOU ARE GRATEFUL FOR AND WHY:

_____

_____

_____

ONE GOAL YOU'D LIKE TO ACCOMPLISH TODAY
(EMOTIONAL OR MENTAL STATE):

_____

_____

Spend 15-20 minutes in meditation on the things you just wrote.
Initial here when you're done. _____

Spend at least 30 minutes consuming positive media (inspirational podcasts, books, videos, etc.). *Initial here when you're done.* _____

👑 NIGHTLY SELF-CARE INVESTMENT

Describe an instance where someone or something attempted to take control of your energy and you did **not** allow it. etc.).
Initial here when you're done. _____

ONE THING YOU'RE PROUD OF YOURSELF FOR DOING TODAY IS:

_____

NOTE: Shut down all social media, TVs, and Netflix at least two hours before bed. Your mind being able to slow down before you go to sleep is critical to its ability to effectively recharge and handle the tasks of the next day.

WEEKLY SCORE CARD

WROTE DOWN AFFIRMATION

_____: _____/7 =

MON   TUES   WED   THURS   FRI   SAT   SUN

WROTE DOWN GOALS

_____: _____/7 =

MON   TUES   WED   THURS   FRI   SAT   SUN

MEDITATED FOR FULL 15-20 MINUTES

_____: _____/7 =

MON   TUES   WED   THURS   FRI   SAT   SUN

CONSUMED POSITIVE MEDIA FOR FULL 30+ MINUTES

_____: _____/7 =

MON   TUES   WED   THURS   FRI   SAT   SUN

COMPLETED NIGHTLY SELF-CARE

_____: _____/7 =

MON   TUES   WED   THURS   FRI   SAT   SUN

WEEKLY SCORE CARD

WHAT HELPED YOU ACHIEVE 100% ON ALL SELF-LOVE INVESTMENTS, AND IF YOU DIDN'T, WHAT DO YOU BELIEVE HINDERED YOU?

_____

_____

WHAT WILL YOU DO TO ACHIEVE 100% NEXT WEEK?

_____

_____

MAJOR TAKEAWAY FROM THIS PAST WEEK THAT YOU'VE LEARNED ABOUT YOURSELF OR LIFE IN GENERAL?

_____

_____

ONE THING THAT HELPS YOU FEEL YOUR ABSOLUTE BEST THIS PAST WEEK:

_____

_____

ONE THING THAT MADE YOU FEEL NOT SO GREAT THIS PAST WEEK:

_____

_____

NAME A WAY YOU WILL CONQUER THAT THING THAT PREVENTED YOU FROM FEELING YOUR BEST.

_____

_____

WEEK 10

MONDAY

TODAY'S AFFIRMATION:

_____

_____

THREE THINGS YOU ARE GRATEFUL FOR AND WHY:

_____

_____

_____

ONE GOAL YOU'D LIKE TO ACCOMPLISH TODAY
(EMOTIONAL OR MENTAL STATE):

_____

_____

Spend 15-20 minutes in meditation on the things you just wrote.
Initial here when you're done. _____

Spend at least 30 minutes consuming positive media (inspirational podcasts,
books, videos, etc.). _Initial here when you're done._ _____

👑 NIGHTLY SELF-CARE INVESTMENT

Describe an instance where someone or something attempted to take control
of your energy and you did _not_ allow it. etc.).
Initial here when you're done. _____

ONE THING YOU'RE PROUD OF YOURSELF FOR DOING TODAY IS:

_____

NOTE: Shut down all social media, TVs, and Netflix at least two hours before bed.
Your mind being able to slow down before you go to sleep is critical to its ability to
effectively recharge and handle the tasks of the next day.

TODAY'S AFFIRMATION:

_____

_____

THREE THINGS YOU ARE GRATEFUL FOR AND WHY:

_____

_____

_____

ONE GOAL YOU'D LIKE TO ACCOMPLISH TODAY
(EMOTIONAL OR MENTAL STATE):

_____

_____

Spend 15-20 minutes in meditation on the things you just wrote.
Initial here when you're done. _____

Spend at least 30 minutes consuming positive media (inspirational podcasts, books, videos, etc.). *Initial here when you're done.* _____

⚜ NIGHTLY SELF-CARE INVESTMENT

Describe an instance where someone or something attempted to take control of your energy and you did *not* allow it. etc.).
Initial here when you're done. _____

ONE THING YOU'RE PROUD OF YOURSELF FOR DOING TODAY IS:

_____

NOTE: Shut down all social media, TVs, and Netflix at least two hours before bed. Your mind being able to slow down before you go to sleep is critical to its ability to effectively recharge and handle the tasks of the next day.

WEDNESDAY

TODAY'S AFFIRMATION:

_____

_____

THREE THINGS YOU ARE GRATEFUL FOR AND WHY:

_____

_____

_____

ONE GOAL YOU'D LIKE TO ACCOMPLISH TODAY
(EMOTIONAL OR MENTAL STATE):

_____

_____

Spend 15-20 minutes in meditation on the things you just wrote.
Initial here when you're done. _____

Spend at least 30 minutes consuming positive media (inspirational podcasts, books, videos, etc.). _Initial here when you're done._ _____

♛ NIGHTLY SELF-CARE INVESTMENT

Describe an instance where someone or something attempted to take control of your energy and you did _not_ allow it. etc.).
Initial here when you're done. _____

ONE THING YOU'RE PROUD OF YOURSELF FOR DOING TODAY IS:

_____

NOTE: Shut down all social media, TVs, and Netflix at least two hours before bed. Your mind being able to slow down before you go to sleep is critical to its ability to effectively recharge and handle the tasks of the next day.

TODAY'S AFFIRMATION:

_____

_____

THREE THINGS YOU ARE GRATEFUL FOR AND WHY:

_____

_____

_____

ONE GOAL YOU'D LIKE TO ACCOMPLISH TODAY
(EMOTIONAL OR MENTAL STATE):

_____

_____

Spend 15-20 minutes in meditation on the things you just wrote.
Initial here when you're done. _____

Spend at least 30 minutes consuming positive media (inspirational podcasts, books, videos, etc.). *Initial here when you're done.* _____

👑 NIGHTLY SELF-CARE INVESTMENT

Describe an instance where someone or something attempted to take control of your energy and you did *not* allow it. etc.).
Initial here when you're done. _____

ONE THING YOU'RE PROUD OF YOURSELF FOR DOING TODAY IS:

_____

NOTE: Shut down all social media, TVs, and Netflix at least two hours before bed. Your mind being able to slow down before you go to sleep is critical to its ability to effectively recharge and handle the tasks of the next day.

FRIDAY

TODAY'S AFFIRMATION:

_____

_____

THREE THINGS YOU ARE GRATEFUL FOR AND WHY:

_____

_____

_____

ONE GOAL YOU'D LIKE TO ACCOMPLISH TODAY
(EMOTIONAL OR MENTAL STATE):

_____

_____

Spend 15-20 minutes in meditation on the things you just wrote.
Initial here when you're done. _____

Spend at least 30 minutes consuming positive media (inspirational podcasts,
books, videos, etc.). *Initial here when you're done.* _____

NIGHTLY SELF-CARE INVESTMENT

Describe an instance where someone or something attempted to take control
of your energy and you did *not* allow it. etc.).
Initial here when you're done. _____

ONE THING YOU'RE PROUD OF YOURSELF FOR DOING TODAY IS:

_____

NOTE: Shut down all social media, TVs, and Netflix at least two hours before bed.
Your mind being able to slow down before you go to sleep is critical to its ability to
effectively recharge and handle the tasks of the next day.

TODAY'S AFFIRMATION:

_____

_____

THREE THINGS YOU ARE GRATEFUL FOR AND WHY:

_____

_____

_____

ONE GOAL YOU'D LIKE TO ACCOMPLISH TODAY
(EMOTIONAL OR MENTAL STATE):

_____

_____

Spend 15-20 minutes in meditation on the things you just wrote.
Initial here when you're done. _____

Spend at least 30 minutes consuming positive media (inspirational podcasts, books, videos, etc.). *Initial here when you're done.* _____

NIGHTLY SELF-CARE INVESTMENT

Describe an instance where someone or something attempted to take control of your energy and you did *not* allow it. etc.).
Initial here when you're done. _____

ONE THING YOU'RE PROUD OF YOURSELF FOR DOING TODAY IS:

_____

NOTE: Shut down all social media, TVs, and Netflix at least two hours before bed. Your mind being able to slow down before you go to sleep is critical to its ability to effectively recharge and handle the tasks of the next day.

SUNDAY

TODAY'S AFFIRMATION:

_____

_____

THREE THINGS YOU ARE GRATEFUL FOR AND WHY:

_____

_____

_____

ONE GOAL YOU'D LIKE TO ACCOMPLISH TODAY
(EMOTIONAL OR MENTAL STATE):

_____

_____

Spend 15-20 minutes in meditation on the things you just wrote.
Initial here when you're done. _____

Spend at least 30 minutes consuming positive media (inspirational podcasts,
books, videos, etc.). _Initial here when you're done._ _____

NIGHTLY SELF-CARE INVESTMENT

Describe an instance where someone or something attempted to take control
of your energy and you did _not_ allow it. etc.).
Initial here when you're done. _____

ONE THING YOU'RE PROUD OF YOURSELF FOR DOING TODAY IS:

_____

NOTE: Shut down all social media, TVs, and Netflix at least two hours before bed.
Your mind being able to slow down before you go to sleep is critical to its ability to
effectively recharge and handle the tasks of the next day.

WEEKLY SCORE CARD

WROTE DOWN AFFIRMATION

_____: ____/7 =

MON   TUES   WED   THURS   FRI   SAT   SUN

WROTE DOWN GOALS

_____: ____/7 =

MON   TUES   WED   THURS   FRI   SAT   SUN

MEDITATED FOR FULL 15-20 MINUTES

_____: ____/7 =

MON   TUES   WED   THURS   FRI   SAT   SUN

CONSUMED POSITIVE MEDIA FOR FULL 30+ MINUTES

_____: ____/7 =

MON   TUES   WED   THURS   FRI   SAT   SUN

COMPLETED NIGHTLY SELF-CARE

_____: ____/7 =

MON   TUES   WED   THURS   FRI   SAT   SUN

WEEKLY SCORE CARD

WHAT HELPED YOU ACHIEVE 100% ON ALL SELF-LOVE
INVESTMENTS, AND IF YOU DIDN'T, WHAT DO YOU
BELIEVE HINDERED YOU?

_____

_____

WHAT WILL YOU DO TO ACHIEVE 100% NEXT WEEK?

_____

_____

MAJOR TAKEAWAY FROM THIS PAST WEEK THAT YOU'VE
LEARNED ABOUT YOURSELF OR LIFE IN GENERAL?

_____

_____

ONE THING THAT HELPS YOU FEEL YOUR ABSOLUTE BEST
THIS PAST WEEK:

_____

_____

ONE THING THAT MADE YOU FEEL NOT SO GREAT THIS
PAST WEEK:

_____

_____

NAME A WAY YOU WILL CONQUER THAT THING THAT
PREVENTED YOU FROM FEELING YOUR BEST.

_____

_____

WEEK 11

MONDAY

TODAY'S AFFIRMATION:

_____

_____

THREE THINGS YOU ARE GRATEFUL FOR AND WHY:

_____

_____

_____

ONE GOAL YOU'D LIKE TO ACCOMPLISH TODAY
(EMOTIONAL OR MENTAL STATE):

_____

_____

Spend 15-20 minutes in meditation on the things you just wrote.
Initial here when you're done. _____

Spend at least 30 minutes consuming positive media (inspirational podcasts,
books, videos, etc.). *Initial here when you're done.* _____

♔ NIGHTLY SELF-CARE INVESTMENT

Describe an instance where someone or something attempted to take control
of your energy and you did ***not*** allow it. etc.).
Initial here when you're done. _____

ONE THING YOU'RE PROUD OF YOURSELF FOR DOING TODAY IS:

_____

NOTE: Shut down all social media, TVs, and Netflix at least two hours before bed.
Your mind being able to slow down before you go to sleep is critical to its ability to
effectively recharge and handle the tasks of the next day.

TODAY'S AFFIRMATION:

_____

_____

THREE THINGS YOU ARE GRATEFUL FOR AND WHY:

_____

_____

_____

ONE GOAL YOU'D LIKE TO ACCOMPLISH TODAY
(EMOTIONAL OR MENTAL STATE):

_____

_____

Spend 15-20 minutes in meditation on the things you just wrote.
Initial here when you're done. _____

Spend at least 30 minutes consuming positive media (inspirational podcasts,
books, videos, etc.). _Initial here when you're done._ _____

NIGHTLY SELF-CARE INVESTMENT

Describe an instance where someone or something attempted to take control
of your energy and you did **not** allow it. etc.).
Initial here when you're done. _____

ONE THING YOU'RE PROUD OF YOURSELF FOR DOING TODAY IS:

_____

NOTE: Shut down all social media, TVs, and Netflix at least two hours before bed.
Your mind being able to slow down before you go to sleep is critical to its ability to
effectively recharge and handle the tasks of the next day.

WEDNESDAY

TODAY'S AFFIRMATION:

_____

_____

THREE THINGS YOU ARE GRATEFUL FOR AND WHY:

_____

_____

_____

ONE GOAL YOU'D LIKE TO ACCOMPLISH TODAY
(EMOTIONAL OR MENTAL STATE):

_____

_____

Spend 15-20 minutes in meditation on the things you just wrote.
Initial here when you're done. _____

Spend at least 30 minutes consuming positive media (inspirational podcasts,
books, videos, etc.). *Initial here when you're done.* _____

NIGHTLY SELF-CARE INVESTMENT

Describe an instance where someone or something attempted to take control
of your energy and you did *not* allow it. etc.).
Initial here when you're done. _____

ONE THING YOU'RE PROUD OF YOURSELF FOR DOING TODAY IS:

_____

NOTE: Shut down all social media, TVs, and Netflix at least two hours before bed.
Your mind being able to slow down before you go to sleep is critical to its ability to
effectively recharge and handle the tasks of the next day.

THURSDAY

TODAY'S AFFIRMATION:

_____

_____

THREE THINGS YOU ARE GRATEFUL FOR AND WHY:

_____

_____

_____

ONE GOAL YOU'D LIKE TO ACCOMPLISH TODAY
(EMOTIONAL OR MENTAL STATE):

_____

_____

Spend 15-20 minutes in meditation on the things you just wrote.
Initial here when you're done. _____

Spend at least 30 minutes consuming positive media (inspirational podcasts,
books, videos, etc.). _Initial here when you're done._ _____

NIGHTLY SELF-CARE INVESTMENT

Describe an instance where someone or something attempted to take control
of your energy and you did _not_ allow it. etc.).
Initial here when you're done. _____

ONE THING YOU'RE PROUD OF YOURSELF FOR DOING TODAY IS:

_____

NOTE: Shut down all social media, TVs, and Netflix at least two hours before bed.
Your mind being able to slow down before you go to sleep is critical to its ability to
effectively recharge and handle the tasks of the next day.

FRIDAY

TODAY'S AFFIRMATION:

_____

_____

THREE THINGS YOU ARE GRATEFUL FOR AND WHY:

_____

_____

_____

ONE GOAL YOU'D LIKE TO ACCOMPLISH TODAY
(EMOTIONAL OR MENTAL STATE):

_____

_____

Spend 15-20 minutes in meditation on the things you just wrote.
Initial here when you're done. _____

Spend at least 30 minutes consuming positive media (inspirational podcasts,
books, videos, etc.). _Initial here when you're done._ _____

♔ NIGHTLY SELF-CARE INVESTMENT

Describe an instance where someone or something attempted to take control
of your energy and you did _not_ allow it. etc.).
Initial here when you're done. _____

ONE THING YOU'RE PROUD OF YOURSELF FOR DOING TODAY IS:

_____

NOTE: Shut down all social media, TVs, and Netflix at least two hours before bed.
Your mind being able to slow down before you go to sleep is critical to its ability to
effectively recharge and handle the tasks of the next day.

TODAY'S AFFIRMATION:

_____

_____

THREE THINGS YOU ARE GRATEFUL FOR AND WHY:

_____

_____

_____

ONE GOAL YOU'D LIKE TO ACCOMPLISH TODAY
(EMOTIONAL OR MENTAL STATE):

_____

_____

Spend 15-20 minutes in meditation on the things you just wrote.
Initial here when you're done. _____

Spend at least 30 minutes consuming positive media (inspirational podcasts,
books, videos, etc.). *Initial here when you're done.* _____

⚜ NIGHTLY SELF-CARE INVESTMENT

Describe an instance where someone or something attempted to take control
of your energy and you did *not* allow it. etc.).
Initial here when you're done. _____

ONE THING YOU'RE PROUD OF YOURSELF FOR DOING TODAY IS:

_____

NOTE: Shut down all social media, TVs, and Netflix at least two hours before bed.
Your mind being able to slow down before you go to sleep is critical to its ability to
effectively recharge and handle the tasks of the next day.

SUNDAY

TODAY'S AFFIRMATION:

_____

_____

THREE THINGS YOU ARE GRATEFUL FOR AND WHY:

_____

_____

_____

ONE GOAL YOU'D LIKE TO ACCOMPLISH TODAY
(EMOTIONAL OR MENTAL STATE):

_____

_____

Spend 15-20 minutes in meditation on the things you just wrote.
Initial here when you're done. _____

Spend at least 30 minutes consuming positive media (inspirational podcasts,
books, videos, etc.). _Initial here when you're done._ _____

NIGHTLY SELF-CARE INVESTMENT

Describe an instance where someone or something attempted to take control
of your energy and you did _not_ allow it. etc.).
Initial here when you're done. _____

ONE THING YOU'RE PROUD OF YOURSELF FOR DOING TODAY IS:

_____

NOTE: Shut down all social media, TVs, and Netflix at least two hours before bed.
Your mind being able to slow down before you go to sleep is critical to its ability to
effectively recharge and handle the tasks of the next day.

WEEKLY SCORE CARD

WROTE DOWN AFFIRMATION

_____: ____/7 =

MON   TUES   WED   THURS   FRI   SAT   SUN

WROTE DOWN GOALS

_____: ____/7 =

MON   TUES   WED   THURS   FRI   SAT   SUN

MEDITATED FOR FULL 15-20 MINUTES

_____: ____/7 =

MON   TUES   WED   THURS   FRI   SAT   SUN

CONSUMED POSITIVE MEDIA FOR FULL 30+ MINUTES

_____: ____/7 =

MON   TUES   WED   THURS   FRI   SAT   SUN

COMPLETED NIGHTLY SELF-CARE

_____: ____/7 =

MON   TUES   WED   THURS   FRI   SAT   SUN

WEEKLY SCORE CARD

WHAT HELPED YOU ACHIEVE 100% ON ALL SELF-LOVE
INVESTMENTS, AND IF YOU DIDN'T, WHAT DO YOU
BELIEVE HINDERED YOU?

_____

_____

WHAT WILL YOU DO TO ACHIEVE 100% NEXT WEEK?

_____

_____

MAJOR TAKEAWAY FROM THIS PAST WEEK THAT YOU'VE
LEARNED ABOUT YOURSELF OR LIFE IN GENERAL?

_____

_____

ONE THING THAT HELPS YOU FEEL YOUR ABSOLUTE BEST
THIS PAST WEEK:

_____

_____

ONE THING THAT MADE YOU FEEL NOT SO GREAT THIS
PAST WEEK:

_____

_____

NAME A WAY YOU WILL CONQUER THAT THING THAT
PREVENTED YOU FROM FEELING YOUR BEST.

_____

_____

WEEK 12

MONDAY

TODAY'S AFFIRMATION:

_____

_____

THREE THINGS YOU ARE GRATEFUL FOR AND WHY:

_____

_____

_____

ONE GOAL YOU'D LIKE TO ACCOMPLISH TODAY
(EMOTIONAL OR MENTAL STATE):

_____

_____

Spend 15-20 minutes in meditation on the things you just wrote.
Initial here when you're done. _____

Spend at least 30 minutes consuming positive media (inspirational podcasts,
books, videos, etc.). *Initial here when you're done.* _____

NIGHTLY SELF-CARE INVESTMENT

Describe an instance where someone or something attempted to take control
of your energy and you did **not** allow it. etc.).
Initial here when you're done. _____

ONE THING YOU'RE PROUD OF YOURSELF FOR DOING TODAY IS:

_____

NOTE: Shut down all social media, TVs, and Netflix at least two hours before bed.
Your mind being able to slow down before you go to sleep is critical to its ability to
effectively recharge and handle the tasks of the next day.

TUESDAY

TODAY'S AFFIRMATION:

_____

_____

THREE THINGS YOU ARE GRATEFUL FOR AND WHY:

_____

_____

_____

ONE GOAL YOU'D LIKE TO ACCOMPLISH TODAY
(EMOTIONAL OR MENTAL STATE):

_____

_____

Spend 15-20 minutes in meditation on the things you just wrote.
Initial here when you're done. _____

Spend at least 30 minutes consuming positive media (inspirational podcasts,
books, videos, etc.). *Initial here when you're done.* _____

NIGHTLY SELF-CARE INVESTMENT

Describe an instance where someone or something attempted to take control
of your energy and you did *not* allow it. etc.).
Initial here when you're done. _____

ONE THING YOU'RE PROUD OF YOURSELF FOR DOING TODAY IS:

_____

NOTE: Shut down all social media, TVs, and Netflix at least two hours before bed.
Your mind being able to slow down before you go to sleep is critical to its ability to
effectively recharge and handle the tasks of the next day.

WEDNESDAY

TODAY'S AFFIRMATION:

_____

_____

THREE THINGS YOU ARE GRATEFUL FOR AND WHY:

_____

_____

_____

ONE GOAL YOU'D LIKE TO ACCOMPLISH TODAY
(EMOTIONAL OR MENTAL STATE):

_____

_____

Spend 15-20 minutes in meditation on the things you just wrote.
Initial here when you're done. _____

Spend at least 30 minutes consuming positive media (inspirational podcasts,
books, videos, etc.). *Initial here when you're done.* _____

NIGHTLY SELF-CARE INVESTMENT

Describe an instance where someone or something attempted to take control
of your energy and you did *not* allow it. etc.).
Initial here when you're done. _____

ONE THING YOU'RE PROUD OF YOURSELF FOR DOING TODAY IS:

_____

NOTE: Shut down all social media, TVs, and Netflix at least two hours before bed.
Your mind being able to slow down before you go to sleep is critical to its ability to
effectively recharge and handle the tasks of the next day.

THURSDAY

TODAY'S AFFIRMATION:

_____

_____

THREE THINGS YOU ARE GRATEFUL FOR AND WHY:

_____

_____

_____

ONE GOAL YOU'D LIKE TO ACCOMPLISH TODAY
(EMOTIONAL OR MENTAL STATE):

_____

_____

Spend 15-20 minutes in meditation on the things you just wrote.
Initial here when you're done. _____

Spend at least 30 minutes consuming positive media (inspirational podcasts, books, videos, etc.). _Initial here when you're done._ _____

♛ NIGHTLY SELF-CARE INVESTMENT

Describe an instance where someone or something attempted to take control of your energy and you did _not_ allow it. etc.).
Initial here when you're done. _____

ONE THING YOU'RE PROUD OF YOURSELF FOR DOING TODAY IS:

_____

NOTE: Shut down all social media, TVs, and Netflix at least two hours before bed. Your mind being able to slow down before you go to sleep is critical to its ability to effectively recharge and handle the tasks of the next day.

FRIDAY

TODAY'S AFFIRMATION:

_____

_____

THREE THINGS YOU ARE GRATEFUL FOR AND WHY:

_____

_____

_____

ONE GOAL YOU'D LIKE TO ACCOMPLISH TODAY
(EMOTIONAL OR MENTAL STATE):

_____

_____

Spend 15-20 minutes in meditation on the things you just wrote.
Initial here when you're done. _____

Spend at least 30 minutes consuming positive media (inspirational podcasts,
books, videos, etc.). _Initial here when you're done._ _____

NIGHTLY SELF-CARE INVESTMENT

Describe an instance where someone or something attempted to take control
of your energy and you did *not* allow it. etc.).
Initial here when you're done. _____

ONE THING YOU'RE PROUD OF YOURSELF FOR DOING TODAY IS:

_____

NOTE: Shut down all social media, TVs, and Netflix at least two hours before bed.
Your mind being able to slow down before you go to sleep is critical to its ability to
effectively recharge and handle the tasks of the next day.

TODAY'S AFFIRMATION:

_____

_____

THREE THINGS YOU ARE GRATEFUL FOR AND WHY:

_____

_____

_____

ONE GOAL YOU'D LIKE TO ACCOMPLISH TODAY
(EMOTIONAL OR MENTAL STATE):

_____

_____

Spend 15-20 minutes in meditation on the things you just wrote.
Initial here when you're done. _____

Spend at least 30 minutes consuming positive media (inspirational podcasts,
books, videos, etc.). _Initial here when you're done._ _____

NIGHTLY SELF-CARE INVESTMENT

Describe an instance where someone or something attempted to take control
of your energy and you did **not** allow it. etc.).
Initial here when you're done. _____

ONE THING YOU'RE PROUD OF YOURSELF FOR DOING TODAY IS:

_____

NOTE: Shut down all social media, TVs, and Netflix at least two hours before bed.
Your mind being able to slow down before you go to sleep is critical to its ability to
effectively recharge and handle the tasks of the next day.

SUNDAY

TODAY'S AFFIRMATION:

_____

_____

THREE THINGS YOU ARE GRATEFUL FOR AND WHY:

_____

_____

_____

ONE GOAL YOU'D LIKE TO ACCOMPLISH TODAY
(EMOTIONAL OR MENTAL STATE):

_____

_____

Spend 15-20 minutes in meditation on the things you just wrote.
Initial here when you're done. _____

Spend at least 30 minutes consuming positive media (inspirational podcasts, books, videos, etc.). _Initial here when you're done._ _____

NIGHTLY SELF-CARE INVESTMENT

Describe an instance where someone or something attempted to take control of your energy and you did _not_ allow it. etc.).
Initial here when you're done. _____

ONE THING YOU'RE PROUD OF YOURSELF FOR DOING TODAY IS:

_____

NOTE: Shut down all social media, TVs, and Netflix at least two hours before bed. Your mind being able to slow down before you go to sleep is critical to its ability to effectively recharge and handle the tasks of the next day.

WEEKLY SCORE CARD

WROTE DOWN AFFIRMATION

_____: ____/7 =

MON   TUES   WED   THURS   FRI   SAT   SUN

WROTE DOWN GOALS

_____: ____/7 =

MON   TUES   WED   THURS   FRI   SAT   SUN

MEDITATED FOR FULL 15-20 MINUTES

_____: ____/7 =

MON   TUES   WED   THURS   FRI   SAT   SUN

CONSUMED POSITIVE MEDIA FOR FULL 30+ MINUTES

_____: ____/7 =

MON   TUES   WED   THURS   FRI   SAT   SUN

COMPLETED NIGHTLY SELF-CARE

_____: ____/7 =

MON   TUES   WED   THURS   FRI   SAT   SUN

WEEKLY SCORE CARD

WHAT HELPED YOU ACHIEVE 100% ON ALL SELF-LOVE
INVESTMENTS, AND IF YOU DIDN'T, WHAT DO YOU
BELIEVE HINDERED YOU?

_____

_____

WHAT WILL YOU DO TO ACHIEVE 100% NEXT WEEK?

_____

_____

MAJOR TAKEAWAY FROM THIS PAST WEEK THAT YOU'VE
LEARNED ABOUT YOURSELF OR LIFE IN GENERAL?

_____

_____

ONE THING THAT HELPS YOU FEEL YOUR ABSOLUTE BEST
THIS PAST WEEK:

_____

_____

ONE THING THAT MADE YOU FEEL NOT SO GREAT THIS
PAST WEEK:

_____

_____

NAME A WAY YOU WILL CONQUER THAT THING THAT
PREVENTED YOU FROM FEELING YOUR BEST.

_____

_____

WEEK 13RQ

MONDAY

TODAY'S AFFIRMATION:

_____

_____

THREE THINGS YOU ARE GRATEFUL FOR AND WHY:

_____

_____

_____

ONE GOAL YOU'D LIKE TO ACCOMPLISH TODAY
(EMOTIONAL OR MENTAL STATE):

_____

_____

Spend 15-20 minutes in meditation on the things you just wrote.
Initial here when you're done. _____

Spend at least 30 minutes consuming positive media (inspirational podcasts, books, videos, etc.). _Initial here when you're done._ _____

👑 NIGHTLY SELF-CARE INVESTMENT

Describe an instance where someone or something attempted to take control of your energy and you did _not_ allow it. etc.).
Initial here when you're done. _____

ONE THING YOU'RE PROUD OF YOURSELF FOR DOING TODAY IS:

_____

NOTE: Shut down all social media, TVs, and Netflix at least two hours before bed. Your mind being able to slow down before you go to sleep is critical to its ability to effectively recharge and handle the tasks of the next day.

TUESDAY

TODAY'S AFFIRMATION:

_____

_____

THREE THINGS YOU ARE GRATEFUL FOR AND WHY:

_____

_____

_____

ONE GOAL YOU'D LIKE TO ACCOMPLISH TODAY
(EMOTIONAL OR MENTAL STATE):

_____

_____

Spend 15-20 minutes in meditation on the things you just wrote.
Initial here when you're done. _____

Spend at least 30 minutes consuming positive media (inspirational podcasts,
books, videos, etc.). _Initial here when you're done._ _____

NIGHTLY SELF-CARE INVESTMENT

Describe an instance where someone or something attempted to take control
of your energy and you did **not** allow it. etc.).
Initial here when you're done. _____

ONE THING YOU'RE PROUD OF YOURSELF FOR DOING TODAY IS:

_____

NOTE: Shut down all social media, TVs, and Netflix at least two hours before bed.
Your mind being able to slow down before you go to sleep is critical to its ability to
effectively recharge and handle the tasks of the next day.

WEDNESDAY

_____

_____

THREE THINGS YOU ARE GRATEFUL FOR AND WHY:

_____

_____

_____

ONE GOAL YOU'D LIKE TO ACCOMPLISH TODAY
(EMOTIONAL OR MENTAL STATE):

_____

_____

Spend 15-20 minutes in meditation on the things you just wrote.
Initial here when you're done. _____

Spend at least 30 minutes consuming positive media (inspirational podcasts, books, videos, etc.). _Initial here when you're done._ _____

👑 NIGHTLY SELF-CARE INVESTMENT

Describe an instance where someone or something attempted to take control of your energy and you did _not_ allow it. etc.).
Initial here when you're done. _____

ONE THING YOU'RE PROUD OF YOURSELF FOR DOING TODAY IS:

_____

NOTE: Shut down all social media, TVs, and Netflix at least two hours before bed. Your mind being able to slow down before you go to sleep is critical to its ability to effectively recharge and handle the tasks of the next day.

THURSDAY

TODAY'S AFFIRMATION:

_____

_____

THREE THINGS YOU ARE GRATEFUL FOR AND WHY:

_____

_____

_____

ONE GOAL YOU'D LIKE TO ACCOMPLISH TODAY
(EMOTIONAL OR MENTAL STATE):

_____

_____

Spend 15-20 minutes in meditation on the things you just wrote.
Initial here when you're done. _____

Spend at least 30 minutes consuming positive media (inspirational podcasts,
books, videos, etc.). _Initial here when you're done._ _____

⚜ NIGHTLY SELF-CARE INVESTMENT

Describe an instance where someone or something attempted to take control
of your energy and you did _not_ allow it. etc.).
Initial here when you're done. _____

ONE THING YOU'RE PROUD OF YOURSELF FOR DOING TODAY IS:

_____

NOTE: Shut down all social media, TVs, and Netflix at least two hours before bed.
Your mind being able to slow down before you go to sleep is critical to its ability to
effectively recharge and handle the tasks of the next day.

FRIDAY

_____

_____

THREE THINGS YOU ARE GRATEFUL FOR AND WHY:

_____

_____

_____

ONE GOAL YOU'D LIKE TO ACCOMPLISH TODAY
(EMOTIONAL OR MENTAL STATE):

_____

_____

Spend 15-20 minutes in meditation on the things you just wrote.
Initial here when you're done. _____

Spend at least 30 minutes consuming positive media (inspirational podcasts, books, videos, etc.). *Initial here when you're done.* _____

☙ NIGHTLY SELF-CARE INVESTMENT

Describe an instance where someone or something attempted to take control of your energy and you did *not* allow it. etc.).
Initial here when you're done. _____

ONE THING YOU'RE PROUD OF YOURSELF FOR DOING TODAY IS:

_____

NOTE: Shut down all social media, TVs, and Netflix at least two hours before bed. Your mind being able to slow down before you go to sleep is critical to its ability to effectively recharge and handle the tasks of the next day.

TODAY'S AFFIRMATION:

_____

_____

THREE THINGS YOU ARE GRATEFUL FOR AND WHY:

_____

_____

_____

ONE GOAL YOU'D LIKE TO ACCOMPLISH TODAY
(EMOTIONAL OR MENTAL STATE):

_____

_____

Spend 15-20 minutes in meditation on the things you just wrote.
Initial here when you're done. _____

Spend at least 30 minutes consuming positive media (inspirational podcasts, books, videos, etc.). _Initial here when you're done._ _____

NIGHTLY SELF-CARE INVESTMENT

Describe an instance where someone or something attempted to take control of your energy and you did **not** allow it. etc.).
Initial here when you're done. _____

ONE THING YOU'RE PROUD OF YOURSELF FOR DOING TODAY IS:

_____

NOTE: Shut down all social media, TVs, and Netflix at least two hours before bed. Your mind being able to slow down before you go to sleep is critical to its ability to effectively recharge and handle the tasks of the next day.

SUNDAY

TODAY'S AFFIRMATION:

_____

_____

THREE THINGS YOU ARE GRATEFUL FOR AND WHY:

_____

_____

_____

ONE GOAL YOU'D LIKE TO ACCOMPLISH TODAY
(EMOTIONAL OR MENTAL STATE):

_____

_____

Spend 15-20 minutes in meditation on the things you just wrote.
Initial here when you're done. _____

Spend at least 30 minutes consuming positive media (inspirational podcasts,
books, videos, etc.). _Initial here when you're done._ _____

NIGHTLY SELF-CARE INVESTMENT

Describe an instance where someone or something attempted to take control
of your energy and you did **not** allow it. etc.).
Initial here when you're done. _____

ONE THING YOU'RE PROUD OF YOURSELF FOR DOING TODAY IS:

_____

NOTE: Shut down all social media, TVs, and Netflix at least two hours before bed.
Your mind being able to slow down before you go to sleep is critical to its ability to
effectively recharge and handle the tasks of the next day.

WROTE DOWN AFFIRMATION

_____: ____/7 =

MON   TUES   WED   THURS   FRI   SAT   SUN

WROTE DOWN GOALS

_____: ____/7 =

MON   TUES   WED   THURS   FRI   SAT   SUN

MEDITATED FOR FULL 15-20 MINUTES

_____: ____/7 =

MON   TUES   WED   THURS   FRI   SAT   SUN

CONSUMED POSITIVE MEDIA
FOR FULL 30+ MINUTES

_____: ____/7 =

MON   TUES   WED   THURS   FRI   SAT   SUN

COMPLETED NIGHTLY SELF-CARE

_____: ____/7 =

MON   TUES   WED   THURS   FRI   SAT   SUN

WEEKLY SCORE CARD

WHAT HELPED YOU ACHIEVE 100% ON ALL SELF-LOVE INVESTMENTS, AND IF YOU DIDN'T, WHAT DO YOU BELIEVE HINDERED YOU?

_____

_____

WHAT WILL YOU DO TO ACHIEVE 100% NEXT WEEK?

_____

_____

MAJOR TAKEAWAY FROM THIS PAST WEEK THAT YOU'VE LEARNED ABOUT YOURSELF OR LIFE IN GENERAL?

_____

_____

ONE THING THAT HELPS YOU FEEL YOUR ABSOLUTE BEST THIS PAST WEEK:

_____

_____

ONE THING THAT MADE YOU FEEL NOT SO GREAT THIS PAST WEEK:

_____

_____

NAME A WAY YOU WILL CONQUER THAT THING THAT PREVENTED YOU FROM FEELING YOUR BEST.

_____

_____

CONCLUSION

Congratulations! You've officially completed the jump-start to a life of daily, unapologetic, and intentional self-love. The same way your body needs daily nutrition and your job requires regular attendance, your soul needs you to show up daily and even hourly with something to pour into it or protect it from.

The Self-Crowned Journal has guided you in that direction, given you the foundation you need, and now it's time for you to continue the rest of this journey on your own. If you were still growing from this set of daily tasks, feel free to grab another Self-Crowned Journal, or if you're ready for new areas to build in, write out a different curriculum for yourself to go by. But whatever you do, KEEP GOING!

This is not just a one-and-done thing. This must be a part of your life in order to keep your cup full. This is also a great time to add more resources to your tool belt. Think about the types of programs you can involve yourself in, new endeavors to embark on, new online or local groups to join, books to read, changes to your diet, places to travel, etc. that can keep you discovering ways to increasingly love yourself. Earnestly seek out those things, spaces, and relationships, and embrace them. *You are officially self-crowned, and every step from this point forward is another precious jewel to represent your royalty.*

Self-Crowning Habits to Form and Break

Habits to Break

- Negative self-talk

- Over-carrying burdens of others

- Spending too much time on social media

- Comparing yourself to others

- Responding to negative comments/messages

- Overthinking

- Not going to bed on time

- Procrastinating on starting the day

- Not budgeting money

- Looking at exes' social media

Habits to Form

- Writing in your journal

- Complimenting others

- Complimenting yourself in the mirror

- Making your bed

- Working out

- Making sleep a top priority

- Drinking more water

- Forgiving people without apologies given

- Donating to a cause

- Doing things that both intrigue you and may make you uncomfortable

- Giving to the less fortunate (money or your time)

- Prayer

CPSIA information can be obtained
at www.ICGtesting.com
Printed in the USA
FFHW022309090219
50441616-55642FF